Rude Awakening

Rude Awakening

Threats to the Global Liberal Order

Mauro F. Guillén

PENN

UNIVERSITY OF PENNSYLVANIA PRESS

PHILADELPHIA

Published by
University of Pennsylvania Press
Philadelphia, Pennsylvania 19104-4112

www.upenn.edu/pennpress

Printed in the United States of America on acid-free paper
10 9 8 7 6 5 4 3 2 1

A Cataloging-in-Publication record is available from the Library of
Congress
ISBN 978-0-8122-5044-2

Contents

Preface

Writing a book is a way of coming to terms with a topic. I had difficulty understanding why in recent years so many people turned away from the principles of liberalism. After the collapse of the Soviet Union, the spread of democracy, and the successes of the market economy in at least some parts of the emerging world, it seemed to me that liberal economic and political ideas had demonstrated their power to deliver better standards of living in a free society. The most recent financial crisis, the rise of inequality, and the proliferation of political corruption quickly came to my mind as important reasons why many felt disenchanted. It seemed to me that technological change also played a role in the increasing economic and social dislocation all around us.

I was puzzled and concerned by the growth of parties on the Far Right and the radical Left of the political spectrum, and by how quickly so many voters flocked to populist and nationalist proposals, shunning traditional parties and the political establishment. I had an overwhelming sense that we were approaching the end of an era guided by liberal principles.

Preface

I would not have written this book, thus failing to come to terms with the crisis of the Global Liberal Order, had Eric Halpern and Peter Agree of the University of Pennsylvania Press not approached me with an irresistible offer to write one. I did not hesitate for a second, deciding to take on the challenge without realizing how complex and mercurial global politics have become. I am grateful to them, especially for providing me with some clear guidelines as to how to focus the analysis on the most critical elements of the problem. As always, my wife Sandra and my daughters Daniela and Andrea tolerated my long hours of writing, and gave me some very good ideas to pursue.

How Did We End Up Here?

The Global Liberal Order has underpinned international relations for more than three generations. Born in the wake of World War II, it promised rising living standards and political freedoms for all. Liberalism represented a fundamental bet on the virtues of democracy and the market economy, as imperfect as they both tend to be under some circumstances. It helped turn North America, Western Europe, and Japan into prosperous societies, each with a large and vibrant middle class, and a social safety net. It also brought some of those benefits to other parts of the world, albeit much less systematically. Progress was far from a straight line. The road was indeed winding and bumpy, as illustrated by the struggle for civil rights for minorities and women, the process of decolonization, the oil shocks and economic recessions of the 1970s, and the partial incorporation of the former Soviet republics, Russia, and China into the global economy. According to its defenders, the liberal order brought optimism to the world after the destruction and dislocation of the war.

However, it seems as if liberalism has run out of steam and failed to spread its benefits evenly across everyone in any one society and around the world. Much of the skepticism or outright rejection of liberal ideas nowadays is part of the fallout from an event that apparently took most people by surprise. No challenge to the Global Liberal Order has proven to be as formidable as the global financial crisis and Great Recession of 2008. Rising inequality and the declining legitimacy of established political parties, politicians, and technocratic elites have created a radically new situation. Unexpected results at the polls—from the rise of right-wing extremism in Europe to the Brexit referendum and the election of Donald Trump—ushered in new political realities. Nationalism and populism proliferated both on the right and the left of the spectrum, as in a pincer movement cutting off the political middle ground. Politics are more polarized than ever. Political parties have become confrontational rather than collaborative as they try to protect their voter base.

In the wake of the crisis, liberalism is understood to be the cause of most problems thought to afflict society and the economy. It is blamed for bringing about economic decay, expanding the gulf between the haves and the have-nots, undermining national identity and pride, and enhancing a growing sense of insecurity. It also stands accused of making people turn away from religion and piety. It was attacked as being soft on terrorism, overly permissive on immigration, and misguided in its tolerance of different practices of sexuality. If these criticisms seem incompatible with one another, there is a good reason for it: liberalism found itself in the crossfire between ferocious critics on the right and equally merciless detractors from the left. While not all of them were always illiberal, they certainly became antiliberal, and especially antiestablishment. The reaction against liberalism, both from the Right and the Left, has aimed at the actions of the established political parties, the bureaucrats and technocrats in the government, the business and financial tycoons, even the cultural and media elites.

Most importantly, the crisis has turned a key advantage of liberalism into its most critical weakness. Liberal democracy and the liberal market economy were supposed to broaden and enrich the middle class, which became the backbone of the Global Liberal Order as its key beneficiary and thus its most important constituency. Europe, the United States, and Japan built their postwar economies and political systems on the basis of a vibrant, productive, and happy middle class. No sooner had the growth of the middle class stagnated than liberalism met its most formidable problem: persuading people that a better future lies ahead. The crisis of 2008 and its aftermath suggested that the current generation of young people might not enjoy better standards of living than their parents. That was a reckoning that felt unbearable to a middle class used to a progressive improvement of its lot, however sharp the short-term economic ups and downs due to cyclical recessions.

In the minds of middle-class voters, the reversal of fortune they experienced was not just the result of impersonal market forces. They felt let down by the political and economic establishment, who had abandoned them to their fate. Voters reserved their most vitriolic anger for the financial elites, whom they thought had simply enriched themselves at their expense. Resentful and hungry for solutions, sizable numbers of voters lent their support to radical politicians, either on the Right or the Left. They turned against liberalism, especially against the established parties and the ruling class. They did not expect or wish illiberal policies to become the norm, but they wanted to send a clear message and to experiment with alternatives.

An important aspect of this political turn of events was the historical transformation of the mindset of blue-collar workers, who in Europe and the United States had ceased to be members of the working class to fully buy into the values of the middle class. The decline of manufacturing left them perplexed as they witnessed how their standards of living decreased relative to other groups, and in many cases in absolute terms due to job losses. Economic decline is incompatible with the idea of belonging to the middle class. Intriguingly, these workers and their families turned to nationalist and populist movements on either the Left or the Right, depending on the country, abandoning their traditional support for labor-based parties. Many young people followed suit, especially in countries afflicted by high unemployment. Politics became polarized and radicalized as nationalism and populism gained support among people whose fortunes had declined.

While these political and economic tensions came to the fore in Europe and in the United States, middle classes enjoyed unprecedented growth in the emerging economies of Asia, and to a lesser extent Africa and Latin America. Hundreds of millions of people, once poor, now purchased apartments and automobiles, took vacations, spent money on branded personal goods, and sent their kids to private schools. They also developed expectations as to what their lives should be like in terms of social achievement and economic consumption. Their newly gained status was the result of decades of hard work. They contributed to building emerging economies that posed a competitive threat to Europe and the United States, even Japan. Thus, in addition to the conflict between the elites and the middle class, the twenty-first century brought to the fore the clash between middle classes in the rich countries and middle classes in the emerging world. One important manifestation of this conflict was the debate over trade protectionism. Should Europe or the United States prevent the goods made by the middle class in Asia from entering their market? Who would benefit from such protectionism? Dynamics involve the middle classes, now at a global level, in global economic and political debates.

All economies and all workers were also shaken by technological change. Automation and other kinds of labor-saving innovations, the emergent sharing economy, and mobile telecommunications revolutionized production and consumption. Improving technology provided for a better life, but it also brought major disruptions and considerable job losses. The effects were hardest on specific industries clustered in the so-called Rust Belt of declining industrial towns. In addition, dramatically changing technology altered the dynamics in the political system and in the media, turning the art and the science of political campaigning upside down. Unknown political candidates could now become instant celebrities. The old adage that "name recognition" is fundamental to a political campaign became even more important in the age of Twitter and Facebook.

Meanwhile, migration had once again become a prime topic on the agenda. Immigrants were blamed for everything from job losses to terrorism, and even for cultural decadence. Nativism quickly turned into xenophobia throughout Europe and the United States, with populist politicians exploiting the issue to their advantage. The fact that immigrants tended to have more offspring than the native born added to the atmosphere of fear and doom. The benefits from immigration were brushed aside as people became inclined to scapegoating.

Liberalism came to be associated with all of these negative consequences of trade, capital movements, migration, and technology given that it proposed free movements of goods, services, money, people, and information as the recipe for progress. Advocating for a borderless world became a huge political liability. Championing walls, virtual or real, turned hitherto marginal politicians into front-runners in elections. With opposition to the Global Liberal Order mounting, how could the energy of grassroots movements be harnessed to advance a liberal agenda? What role should political and economic freedoms play in the twenty-first century? Can the Global Liberal Order be reinvented so that it remains useful and relevant?

The Birth of the Global Liberal Order Version 1.0

Let's revisit the basics of how the world was organized before the crisis of 2008. Politics and the economy always need some fundamental rules to unfold successfully. Over the course of history, societies have achieved different forms of government and various ways of organizing the economy. From feudalism and slavery to mercantilism, from central planning to the market economy, countries have constructed a variety of economic systems.

Monarchies and republics, democracies and dictatorships have been adopted as ways to organize polities. We might think of these economic and political arrangements as the "institutional software" that sets the boundaries within which actors can play their roles. The software consists not only of formal laws and regulations but also cultural norms and values, ways of getting things done offered from one generation to the next. No complex society can successfully operate without such arrangements.

The Global Liberal Order was one type of such institutional software designed to organize society and the economy. It proposed to enable everyone to make decisions freely, emphasizing individual rights and obligations subject to stringent constraints to ensure everyone's welfare. Individuals enjoyed a variety of rights, including political rights and property rights. Such rights were central to the functioning of the polity and the economy. A relatively strong role for the state was necessary as the guarantor of such rights and the enforcer of the obligations, and it assumed and relied on the organization of political and economic interests into entities such as political parties, labor unions, and employer associations. Thus, states organized civil society, with these constituents and individuals as their central elements.

The Global Liberal Order came in two different versions. Version 1.0 in this book lasted until the early 1970s. Version 2.0 was meant to help the United States, Europe, and the developing world overcome economic stagnation after the oil shocks in the 1970s by further liberalizing the economy and capital flows, and it was attacked by some as being "neoliberal." In so doing, it paved the road toward a series of crises culminating in the debacle of 2008. Thus,

Version 2.0 ultimately proved to be counterproductive and defective. It became exceedingly complex and failed to deliver the expected results for a variety of reasons.

Political and economic institutions are almost never designed from scratch. They are most distinctively the result of history, culture, tradition, and power struggles among competing interests. Thus, institutional software reflects the very essence of society, and it shapes society as society shapes it. This symbiotic relationship sometimes produces situations in which events spin out of control, leading to partial or total breakdowns.

At its inception, the Global Liberal Order was uniquely designed to deal with an extraordinary set of circumstances. While it certainly built on centuries-long intellectual traditions, and attempted to incorporate building blocks inherited from the past, it achieved a major innovation in terms of the global political and economic architecture. At the end of World War II, the European landscape lay in ruins. Tens of millions had perished, and millions more now searched for food and water amid the rubble. About 15 million people were displaced from their homes as borders were redrawn throughout the continent. The worst genocide in history had just occurred. The Holocaust and the dawn of the nuclear age ushered in a radically new global reality, morally, geopolitically, and economically. East Asia was also reeling from wartime destruction, the restoration of European colonial rule, and the civil war in China. Latin America was far more prosperous than Asia, although just a few benefited. Meanwhile, hundreds of millions throughout the developing world yearned for a better life and for political rights. The United States and the Soviet Union had now launched competing global projects for other countries to join. They made strong appeals, and did not hesitate to use calculated force, overtly or covertly. A new global balance of power emerged from this confrontation.

The efforts orchestrated by the United States and Britain to forge a new global order after World War II emphasized freedom and were the intellectual grandchild of liberalism, both political and economic. They proposed free markets and free trade as the central policy recipe to jump start the economy. Knowing how difficult managing cross-border financial flows can be, they established capital controls and fixed exchange rates. The dollar, a currency barely thirty years old at the time, became the centerpiece of a new global financial architecture, the sun around which all other currencies rotated, with the dollar itself linked to the value of gold.

This financial compartmentalization of the liberal world economy was established as a prerequisite for the successful implementation of a new kind of economic policy, Keynesianism, named after the British economist who theorized it. It essentially involved managing the business cycle by using government taxation and spending to compensate for flagging demand in the economy. Its proponents expected this type of "stop-and-go" fiscal policy making to prevent situations of high unemployment and to bring prosperity to large segments of the population, enlarging and consolidating a vigorous middle class of consumers. The global architecture underpinning this liberal economic order was agreed upon at a famous meeting in 1944, which came to be known as the Bretton Woods framework, named after the New Hampshire resort were the gathering took place.

Chapter 1

Meanwhile, the developing countries, some of which had just gained independence, strived to mature economically by fostering their own manufacturing industries, an effort that had started during the depths of the Depression in some parts of the world, notably Latin America. Developing nations first attempted to replace imports of manufactured goods by promoting domestic production. In order to encourage investment in industry, they protected the domestic market, showering local business with a panoply of subsidies and incentives. Countries as diverse as Argentina, Brazil, Mexico, South Korea, and Taiwan, among many others, pursued this path. While this approach to development—commonly referred to as *import substitution*—yielded some positive results, it eventually ran out of steam given that, as Adam Smith once said, "the division of labor is limited by the extent of the market." Thus, companies inside a protected domestic market could enjoy the benefits of limited competition, but could not achieve the scale and did not find it necessary to innovate in order to survive. The Asian tiger economies of Hong Kong, Singapore, Taiwan, and South Korea were the first to realize that import substitution needed to be supplemented by an export-oriented effort. They successfully transformed themselves into export powerhouses, surging ahead of Latin America in terms of growth and prosperity during the 1960s and 1970s.

While the Bretton Woods agenda, supplemented by the Marshall Plan of 1948 aimed at the reconstruction of the economic infrastructure of Europe, had clear objectives and the means to achieve them, the key geopolitical template of the liberal order did not. This was the Truman Doctrine of 1947, a policy designed to provide economic and military support to countries believed to be threatened by Soviet expansion. The first beneficiaries were Greece and Turkey. This initiative became the driving force behind the formation of the North Atlantic Treaty Organization (NATO) in 1949. The Truman Doctrine amounted to an open-ended and worldwide commitment on the part of the United States "to support free peoples who are resisting attempted subjugation by armed minorities or by outside pressures."[1] In this sense, it sent the United States down the path of intervening in a wide variety of conflicts and civil wars. One cannot really blame President Truman for making such an extraordinary global commitment since he was not planning to be president, had only known Roosevelt for a few months, and was kept in the dark about the existence of a nuclear weapons program. He inherited a situation in which the world looked to the United States for solutions. He provided one.

If the global economy was to be rebuilt around liberal principles, the political side of the global liberal agenda became a bit more complicated to implement. The liberal economic principles of free trade and increasingly free capital flows did not translate well into the political sphere. The reason goes all the way back to the idea of political liberalism. While the logic of the market calls for the removal of barriers between countries, the logic of political liberalism is based on the concept of citizenship, which requires establishing and maintaining national boundaries. Who is a citizen, and who is not, needs to be clarified and upheld in order to determine who has political rights and obligations. Thus, national borders became important demarcations in the liberal world, and not solely in the Soviet bloc.

Chapter 1

The Cold War created a vexing dilemma for the United States and the European colonial powers. Was it justifiable to support dictators who were holding the line against the expansion of communism? Should colonies be allowed to emancipate even when there was a risk of a communist takeover? Might it be better to stage a coup d'état in order to remove a left-leaning elected government than to wait and hope for the best? Did it make sense to postpone democratic transitions until the economy was reorganized and could provide enough opportunities for all? As the superpower confrontation heated up after World War II, these questions were answered in the affirmative in case after case. Support for sitting dictators was supplemented, where necessary, by active involvement in the overthrow of democratically elected governments in Syria, Iran, Guatemala, Lebanon, the Dominican Republic, and Chile, among others. Throughout Asia, Latin America, the Middle East, and Africa, the United States and the former European colonial powers increasingly supported authoritarian rulers, some of them quite brutal in their methods, very much against the principles of political liberalism. Even in the United States, the racial segregation of the South was not just a vestige of the past but a core component of the Faustian bargain struck by the New Dealers as the country transformed itself into a global power.[2]

In sum, the liberal economic and political order championed by the United States since the end of World War II promoted the spread of democracy (except where it was not convenient), free markets, free trade, and increasingly free capital flows. The Truman Doctrine and the Marshall Plan blended nicely with the international financial order that emerged out of the Bretton Woods agreements of 1944. The formula for U.S. engagement with the world became "democracy + free trade + the dollar standard = prosperity," although this mainly applied to the so-called triad of Europe, North America, and Japan. The rest of the world included the dollar area of Latin America (where democracy was dispensable); the Asian, Middle-Eastern, and African colonies of the diminished European powers (which started to fight for their independence); and, of course, the Soviet bloc (which provided the justification for an interventionist international agenda). And the whole setup was under the shadow of the nuclear arms race. As the American writer William Faulkner once put it, people increasingly asked themselves, "When will I be blown up?" Fueled by the Cold War, U.S. military presence around the world grew to well over a thousand facilities in nearly eighty countries.

This state of affairs prevailed throughout the 1950s. By the beginning of the Kennedy presidency in 1960, however, the winds of change were gathering speed, domestically and internationally. The civil rights movement, the divisive Vietnam War, the women's liberation movement, and the process of decolonization created a radically new global reality by the end of the 1960s. At the outset a prosperous economy with a trade surplus, the United States stagnated, unemployment rose, and deficits started to grow. In 1971 President Nixon made the momentous decision to bring dollar convertibility into gold to an end, triggering a succession of monetary and financial crises around the world. The world had also become more complex, at least measured by the number of independent countries. In 1945, the United Nations was founded by 51 sovereign states. By 1960, its membership had grown to 99, and by 1970 to 127.

Decolonization, the end of dollar convertibility into gold, and the oil shocks brought about intense change and plenty of volatility. Proxy wars between the two superpowers proliferated under the guise of civil wars. Looking back at the 1960s, and in spite of the political turmoil, it was seen as the heyday of the Global Liberal Order Version 1.0.

The Global Liberal Order Version 2.0

Responses to the stagnation and inflation of crises of the 1970s brought global economic growth to a halt. The elections of Margaret Thatcher and Ronald Reagan in 1979 and 1980, respectively, represented victory for the view that the role of the state in the economy should be diminished. In addition, they proposed an agenda of financial liberalization, which was forcefully championed by a series of French technocrats at the helm of the International Monetary Fund and the European Union. Together, these politicians and policy makers revamped the global financial architecture created in the postwar settlement, removing barriers to the free movement of capital, and unleashing a new form of global capitalism. In parallel, more countries were brought into the liberal trading system. The bold U.S. alliance with China launched by President Nixon in 1973 may or may have not paved the way to the end of the Cold War, but it certainly gave rise to a new kind of global economy, one that eventually enthroned the U.S. consumer as its pivotal actor. China became the manufacturing workshop of the world, and the United States the most important consumer market.

The Idea of Capital Mobility

Driving global financial reforms was the idea that everyone would benefit from a world in which capital could move freely from wherever it is abundant to wherever it is scarce and needed. The best way to create jobs and accelerate growth, according to this view, was to let capital flow to the locations in the world where the best opportunities exist. While this was an idea with merit, it was implemented in such a way that short-term capital movements became the norm, as money chased the highest returns in a world increasingly characterized by economic, political, and currency risks. Those short-term capital flows did not necessarily create jobs; in fact, they tended instead to make crises, and hence job losses, more frequent. It is fair to say that the Global Liberal Order Version 2.0 represented the elevation of financial interests above all others.[3]

By the turn of the twenty-first century, there were 189 member states of the United Nations; the United States recorded the largest trade deficit and China and Germany the largest surpluses. Capital could freely roam the global economy across a larger number of economies, monetary areas, and tax jurisdictions than ever. Europe had embarked on its adventure to share a single currency, technological change promised a paradise on Earth, and Russia appeared to be yet another country that had joined the Global Liberal Order. It seemed as if one side had won, and that liberalism had triumphed. In fact, the liberal model of democracy seemed to have been adopted around the world. In 1946 only 30 percent of all independent countries were democracies, a proportion that remained fairly stable until the end of the Cold War in 1989, for two reasons. First, the communist regimes were decidedly undemocratic and autocratic. And second, the United States and its allies supported dictatorial regimes throughout the world. This state of affairs changed after the collapse of the Berlin Wall. By 2001, and for the first time in history, more than half of all independent countries were stable democracies, and by 2015 the proportion reached 58 percent.

There were also economic and technological reasons for triumphalism. In spite of the crises that occurred in the emerging markets throughout the 1990s, Europe and the United States managed to overcome short-lived recessions, and continued to offer high standards of living for their populations. This was also an era of technological optimism. The so-called new economy promised growth and prosperity beyond anyone's dreams. People enjoyed a bewildering variety of new gadgets, from smartphones to flat-screen TVs. Globalization in the economic, financial, and technological spheres promised to create opportunities for all and to offer advanced goods at affordable prices. It seemed as if the Global Liberal Order would last forever.

Financial Markets and Financial Innovation

When it came to financial markets, the Reagan, Bush, and Clinton administrations believed in the removal of obstacles to the free unfolding of market forces and in the benefits of sophisticated financial innovations, under the assumption that markets could self-regulate. Their legislative and regulatory initiatives gave rise to Version 2.0 of the Global Liberal Order. In 1986, Margaret Thatcher set into motion a major revolution in financial services with the so-called London Big Bang. This reform should be seen in the context of a package of neoliberal reforms that included the privatization of state-owned enterprises and the deregulation of many other markets. Fixed trading commissions were eliminated, electronic trading introduced, and the cozy club of City insiders was effectively dismantled, opening the brokerage business to competition. Over the next two decades, London regained its long-gone status as the world's leading financial center, attracting the likes of J. P. Morgan, Lehman Brothers, and AIG. The fact that regulatory oversight was less stringent in London than in New York made it a magnet for U.S. financial institutions as a location in which to experiment with new financial products.[4]

Meanwhile, regulatory developments in the United States were creating a more fertile ground for financial innovation and risk taking. In the early 1990s regulators and Congress considered several initiatives and bills to monitor and oversee the expanding universe of derivatives products. Intense industry lobbying caused these initiatives to be shelved. In 1996, with Alan Greenspan at the helm, the Federal Reserve made the astonishing and reckless decision to allow financial institutions to reduce required reserves if they used credit derivatives to curb risks. Perhaps the most prominent piece of legislation from the 1990s was the Financial Services Modernization Act of 1999, which repealed the even more famous

Glass-Steagall Act of 1933 and amended the Bank Holding Company Act of 1954 to permit commercial banks to enter the securities and insurance business and vice versa. Then Treasury Secretary Lawrence Summers explained that "at the end of the 20th century we will at last be replacing an archaic set of restrictions [on financial activity] with a legislative foundation for a 21st century financial system." He asserted that the legislation "would provide significant benefits to the national economy."[5]

Greenspan, Summers, and Robert Rubin—a former manager of Goldman's fixed-income division—opposed new regulations on derivatives, products that enable investors to make bets on the future prices of underlying assets such as bonds, equity shares, commodities, and the like. Such regulations would have made the system safer. The modest recommendation of the Commodity Futures Trading Commission in 1998 to regulate derivatives, including disclosure rules and capital cushions, was ignored. Summers argued that derivatives "serve an important purpose in allocating risk by letting each person take as much of whatever kind of risk he wants." He made the following statement at the U.S. Senate:

> derivatives facilitate domestic and international commerce and support a more efficient allocation of capital across the economy. They can also improve the functioning of financial markets themselves by potentially raising liquidity and narrowing the bid-asked spreads in the underlying cash markets. Thus OTC [over-the-counter] derivatives directly and indirectly support higher investment and growth in living standards in the United States and around the world.[6]

The reforms and deregulation promoted by the Reagan, Bush, and Clinton administrations would have infamous consequences, paving the way to the crisis of 2008. For example, as commercial banks entered the securities business, investment banks felt competitive pressure, triggering a race to the bottom in terms of risk assessment standards.[7] Investment banking became more like gambling rather than a traditional financial activity.

There are many factors that contributed to the dismantling of the Depression-era regulations, among them, international competition, the ideological convergence of the Republican and Democratic parties when it came to economic and financial matters, and changes in the marketplace resulting in a merging of interests among commercial banks, securities firms, and insurance companies. For many years after the Great Depression, American commercial banks operated differently from European banks. Since the early 1980s financial interests argued that Glass-Steagall should be repealed to enable American banks to enter the securities business so as to level the playing field. Though initially the argument emphasized the banks' loss of business to other domestic financial institutions, eventually U.S. banks argued that they could not compete with Japanese banks, which had become among the largest in the world and were able to operate securities firms in the United States. Then in 1986, Thatcher's decision to revolutionize the financial services sector with the London Big Bang put additional international competitive pressure on U.S. policy makers. In 1987 the Reagan administration announced that Treasury had concluded that American banks should be allowed to merge with other financial institutions if they were going to be able to compete in the international arena.[8] In 1989 the Bush White House was also explicit in that international competition was a motivating factor for advocating regulatory change. The argument made at this time was not that U.S. banks could not compete with British banks, but that the City of London had overtaken New York as the financial capital of the world. These competitive pressures coincided with the ideological convergence of the Republican and Democratic parties on a deregulation agenda.[9]

The repeal of Glass-Steagall and amendments to the Bank Holding Company Act occurred with a Republican Congress and a Democratic president. Democrats in Congress had opposed the integration of banking, securities, and insurance businesses in the mid-1980s, but would eventually reverse their position and follow the lead of the Clinton administration. Clinton captured the White House after twelve years of Republican administrations by claiming to be the leader of a new Democratic Party, one that would embrace private sector growth versus the government sector. Clinton's margin of victory over the other contenders for the Democratic Party nomination had allowed him to set a more pro-business agenda than the one advocated by the more traditionally liberal Democratic constituencies. In fact, the Clinton administration supported financial deregulation from the outset. Then when in the 1994 midterm elections the Republican Party won a majority in both the House and Senate, the stage was set for a major overhaul of the Depression-era regulations long advocated by the large commercial banks.

The evolution of business interests with regards to the dismantling of regulations dating back to the 1930s was the result of important changes in the financial markets.

Lobbying, and the accompanying campaign contributions, by commercial banks did not let up. Their efforts were thwarted by the securities and insurance industries, which did not want competition from commercial banks. Legislators were also wary of allowing federally insured commercial banks to merge with other financial firms whose profitability was more volatile. Eventually, the securities industry decided that they end their long-standing opposition to the repeal of Glass-Steagall. In exchange, securities firms wanted to be allowed to expand into commercial banking and have access to the Fed's emergency borrowing, while commercial banks wanted entry into the insurance industry as well and continued to pressure Congress for across-the-board integration of financial services. The passage of the Financial Modernization Act of 1999 thus signaled the end of an era when the fear that financial entities could become "too big to fail" had kept financial deregulators at bay.[10]

The removal of restrictions per se did not necessarily have to spell trouble. After all, many countries around the world allowed integrated and diversified financial firms to operate. Unlike in other countries, however, the U.S. regulatory structure was not overhauled in order to guarantee the stability of this radically transformed financial system. This was arguably the key mistake made by the Clinton administration, later compounded by the lack of oversight during the Bush years leading up to the crisis. Commercial banks continued to be supervised by the Federal Reserve, the Office of the Comptroller of the Currency, the Federal Deposit Insurance Corporation, and individual states. Securities firms were primarily under the watch of the Securities and Exchange Commission (SEC). Insurance companies were regulated by individual states and by the Department of Labor. After 1999, a diversified financial services company was allowed to choose the regulator for each of its businesses, leading to a situation in which no single government body had a 360-degree view of the entire portfolio of each company and the associated systemic interactions. The Commodity Futures Modernization Act of 2000 also added to the problem by treating swaps as distinct from futures or securities. This essentially meant that neither the SEC nor the Commodity Futures Trading Commission (which is overseen by the U.S. Congress Agriculture committee and was explicitly barred by Congress from regulating the over-the-counter derivatives market shortly after the Long-Term Capital Management fiasco!) could supervise these new, and potentially lethal, financial products. Industry lobbying was very effective at obtaining a favorable ruling on the part of the SEC concerning leverage ratios. In 2004 the agency voted to raise them. Not surprisingly, Lehman, Bear Stearns, and Morgan Stanley increased their asset-to-equity ratios above 3,000 percent, and Merrill Lynch and Goldman Sachs above 2,500 percent. The Basel Committee on Banking Supervision, an international entity charged with ensuring that global financial institutions meet certain criteria of financial solidity, also agreed to lower capital ratios. It seemed as if everyone placed a huge bet on the potential benefits of financial deregulation.

The Washington Consensus

While Thatcher, Reagan, and Clinton launched Version 2.0 of the Global Liberal Order, a bunch of influential French technocrats at the International Monetary Fund who were firm believers that free movements of capital would bring prosperity to everyone persuaded countries around the world, or in many cases required them, to adopt capital account liberalization, or free capital flows.[11] This was in fact one of the components of a new policy toolkit that emerged from the International Monetary Fund (IMF) and the World Bank. It was dubbed the "Washington Consensus." The list of policy prescriptions became longer over time and more focused on the business sector and on a retreat of the state from the economy. Fiscal discipline, financial liberalization, openness to trade and investment, privatization, deregulation, and protection of property rights were presented as necessary to create the foundations for sustained economic growth.[12]

The lackluster results of these policies in Latin America and Africa during the 1990s led policy makers to enlarge the agenda to include an even more sweeping list of necessary reforms, including corporate governance, labor market flexibility, independent central banks, and anticorruption measures, among others. This "augmented" Washington Consensus, while theoretically on target, was exceedingly difficult to implement in practice. It placed too much emphasis on eliminating inefficiencies and on the virtues of free financial flows without seriously considering dynamic innovation as the engine of growth. Moreover, the success of this model of economic growth required wholesale institutional reform on several fronts simultaneously, something that would likely be opposed politically by various interest groups, and not always be conducive to superior economic outcomes.[13]

Chapter 1

By the turn of the twenty-first century, criticism of the large-projects approach by the World Bank and institutional reforms by the IMF had become intense, and it came from different quarters, including not only constituencies traditionally skeptical of, or opposed to, such efforts, but also mainstream economists. Dissatisfaction with the policy prescriptions of those multilateral agencies contributed to the overall sense that economic liberalism was not to the benefit of poor or developing countries.

The Mushrooming of Trade Blocs

At the same time that the global economy was becoming more integrated financially, it was also reshaping itself through the formation of trade blocs. The Global Liberal Order Version 1.0 was all about multilateralism, that is, negotiations among a large number of countries to produce agreements fostering freer trade. The General Agreement on Tariffs and Trade (GATT), originally signed in 1947 by twenty-three countries, helped bring down tariff and nontariff barriers to trade during the 1950s and 1960s. By the 1970s, the sheer number of countries involved—over a hundred—meant that negotiations would last years, not months. In fact, the Tokyo round concluded in 1973, more than six years after it was launched. It was at this time that the GATT came to be known as the General Agreement to Talk and Talk. The Uruguay round that ended in 1986 lasted one year longer, bringing about a quantum change in the global trading system by fully incorporating China into it and creating the World Trade Organization (WTO) as the successor to GATT. The latest negotiations, known as the Doha round, were launched in 2001 with 141 countries sitting at the table, and have yet to be concluded.

The intrinsic difficulty of reaching agreements among a large number of countries and the desire to organize trade regionally led to the formation of trade blocs, another key feature that set Version 2.0 of the Global Liberal Order apart from Version 1.0. These agreements involving two or more countries could be as simple as a preferential trade area reducing tariffs for certain goods and as complex and unwieldy as an economic and monetary union such as the Euro Zone, with all shades of grey in between from free trade areas (like the North American Free Trade Agreement [NAFTA]) to customs unions, common markets, and single markets (like the European Union [EU]). By 2017 there were over three hundred trade blocs registered with the WTO, implying that many countries had signed multiple agreements with different sets of countries.[14]

The EU and NAFTA, while starkly different, were the largest trade blocs in the world, and also the two that would find themselves at the center of most of the debates and controversies after the turn of the twenty-first century. NAFTA was essentially a free trade area for merchandise combined with some free trade in services and free capital flows. The EU was far more comprehensive, including free trade in both goods and services, free movement of labor and capital, a coordinated value added tax, and a common regulatory and competition framework. In addition, nineteen of its twenty-seven members agreed to share a single currency, the euro, which was originally launched at the beginning of 1999.

Chapter 1

The Premature Launching of the Euro

Given how central the Euro Zone became to the crisis of 2008 and the subsequent rise of nationalist-populist movements and parties, it is essential to understand the logic behind it. Currencies are a peculiar commodity. Among other things, they are the main way in which an economy adjusts to external shocks. Politically, they are a symbol of a country's stature in the global system. Surrendering monetary authority to the supranational level requires a number preparatory steps regarding the labor market as well as fiscal, financial, and banking policies and regulations.

Adopting a single currency among geographically adjacent countries closely intertwined in terms of trade, capital, labor, and regulations makes perfect sense economic to reduce transaction costs. That was the official reason why the euro was adopted. A single currency, however, was also politically expedient because it would lock governments into a European frame of mind and policy framework.

Besides these economic and political motivations, it is important to realize that sharp currency fluctuations and crises during the 1970s and 1980s created a strong desire among European leaders to take some steps toward financial and monetary coordination. Capital market integration in Europe had long been championed by Germany, Holland, and the United Kingdom, but opposed by France. The election of François Mitterrand in 1981 and his failed Keynesian stimulation of the economy created a very different scenario, one in which elite French policy makers saw capital controls as hopelessly ineffective and punitive to the middle class. The *tournant*, or Mitterrand U-turn, paved the way for the integration of European capital markets and provided ammunition for those in support of taking the ultimate step in unification, the introduction of a common currency.[15] "The euro is fundamentally a political project," argued Barry Eichengreen. "This is its weakness, since it explains how it was that the euro was created before all the economic prerequisites needed for its smooth operation were in place." It is, essentially, "a currency without a state. It is the first major currency not backed by a major government."[16]

Regardless of the economic and political arguments in favor of the single currency, there was widespread agreement in Europe during the 1980s that it would take a long time, perhaps several decades, to put in place the necessary institutions to ensure that a single currency would work well. Europe contained many more differences and was less an "optimal currency area" than the United States. To illustrate the point, it is useful to compare the nineteen countries in the Euro Zone with the fifty states of the United States in terms of four basic criteria. Regarding trade, interstate "exports" in the United States were equivalent to 66 percent of U.S. GDP in 2007, just before the crisis started, compared to just 17 percent for the Euro Zone. In terms of the correlation of local growth between 1997 and 2007, the coefficients were 0.46 and 0.51, respectively. In terms of labor mobility in 2012, 42 percent of Americans were born outside their state of residence, compared to only 17 percent in the Euro Zone. Finally, in terms of fiscal matters, 28 percent of local income in the United States could be offset by federal transfers in the event of a macroeconomic shock versus just 0.5 percent in the case of the Euro Zone. Thus, it would take a long time for a putative Euro Zone to even approximate the levels of integration of the United States.[17]

Chapter 1

The premature introduction of the euro in 1999 owed much to the idiosyncratic characters involved. Prominent among the elite policy makers in favor of more capital integration in Europe was Jacques Delors, Mitterrand's finance minister (1981–84), later to become president of the European Commission (1985–94). Delors was a devout Catholic and a staunch technocrat, a rare combination within the Socialist Party elite. Also in the high echelons of government at the time was Michel Camdessus, later to become deputy governor and governor of the Bank of France, and most famously managing director of the IMF between 1987 and 2000. Delors and Camdessus were the longest-serving officials at the helm of the European Commission and the IMF, respectively. Both of them were elite French civil servants, educated in Paris, and with experience at the country's central bank. Their belief in the benefits of unfettered capital flows became extremely influential in European policy circles and around the world. Their proposals succeeded when European countries agreed to the formation of a single market for goods, services, labor, and capital, which became a reality at the beginning of 1993 with the coming into effect of the Maastricht Treaty.[18] They also believed in a long-standing idea among French technocrats that "Europe will be made of money, or it will not be made," as Jacques Rueff, a central banker and advisor to President Charles de Gaulle, once put it.[19]

After several failed attempts to coordinate monetary and currency policies in Europe, in June 1988 Mitterrand met with German chancellor Helmut Kohl to discuss the prospects for monetary union. The outcome of that meeting was France's commitment to capital flow liberalization and Germany's acquiescence to form a high-level committee to study a future monetary union. Most importantly, however, the Germans did not agree to any specific timetable for currency unification. Still, Mitterrand and Delors pressed on, and the committee—composed of the twelve central bank presidents or governors of the member countries plus three other experts—produced the so-called Delors Report, published in April 1989, establishing a relatively long calendar consisting of the abolition of capital controls by 1990, convergence of macroeconomic policies beginning in 1994, and the definition of the criteria for membership in the eventual monetary union by 1999.[20] "Economic and monetary union," the report stated, "would represent the final result of the process of progressive economic integration in Europe."[21] As political scientist Rawi Abdelal has aptly observed:

> The choice for monetary union appeared to be perfectly logical. Within an asymmetric EMS [European Monetary System], France had only limited monetary autonomy. Monetary policy for all of Europe was essentially made by the Bundesbank in Frankfurt. With monetary union, however, a French central banker would at least have a seat at the table with his or her German and other European colleagues to make monetary policy for all of Europe. . . . As [Jacques] de Larosière, then governor of the Banque de France, put in in 1990, "Today I am governor of a central bank who has decided, along with his nation, to follow fully the German monetary policy without voting on it. At least, as part of a European central bank, I'll have a vote."[22]

The report was a personal triumph for Delors and his fellow technocrats. However, it was clear to them that there would have been no agreement without the support of Karl Otto Pöhl, the powerful president of the Bundesbank, who pressed for budgetary convergence criteria, an independent European Central Bank obligated to maintain price stability, and no transfer of sovereignty at the start. In agreeing to plans for monetary union, Pöhl went against the hardliners within his own central bank.[23] After all, Delors had observed in 1992 that "not all Germans believe in God, but they all believe in the Bundesbank."[24]

Then, on November 9, 1989, the Berlin Wall fell. In December Kohl asked its European partners to support his plan for German unification at a meeting in Strasbourg. For his part, Mitterrand asked the German chancellor to agree to an intergovernmental conference on monetary union to be held the following December, thus accelerating the calendar for the adoption of the common currency by at least two years. French pressure on the Germans resulted in the signing of the Treaty on European Union in December 1991 at Maastricht. Essentially, France wanted a quick transition to monetary union in parallel with German unification while Germany preferred a much longer process prioritizing political union and pursuing monetary union only at a later date.[25] Mitterrand's paramount goal was to ensure that a united Germany would be "embedded in an integrating Europe,"[26] a solution that also pleased Margaret Thatcher, George Bush, and Mikhail Gorbachev. As Timothy Garton Ash famously put it, quoting "a wit," the outcome was "the whole of Deutschland for Kohl, half the deutsche Mark for Mitterrand."[27]

By the turn of the twenty-first century, the global economy was well underway on a path toward greater financial integration, led as always by the United States and the United Kingdom, with France and its technocrats enthusiastically on board, and Germany reluctantly willing to go along. Meanwhile, trade blocs proliferated, the Euro Zone launched the most ambitious monetary experiment ever, and the emerging economies continued to grow rapidly. It was against this rapidly evolving backdrop that the Global Liberal Order Version 2.0 ran into problems eventually leading to the "perfect storm" of 2008.

Chapter 2

The Rude Awakening

No more than two decades after the Global Liberal Order Version 2.0 came into being, the world was ensnared in instability, inequality, and growing economic tensions. Financial and economic crises, new political movements, xenophobia, and unexpected electoral outcomes were some of the byproducts of a highly volatile situation. Politics became partisan, divisive, and polarized.

The first signs of trouble emerged in the mid-1990s. Currency crises spread like wildfire throughout Latin America, East Asia, and the former Soviet Union. The trend toward democracy reversed itself with the rise of a new breed of strongmen in all four corners of the world, from Chávez and Maduro in Venezuela to Mugabe in Zimbabwe, and from Putin in Russia to Assad in Syria and Erdoğan in Turkey. Meanwhile, states lost control over the situation on the ground, especially in sub-Saharan Africa, the Middle East, and South Asia, in what became to be known as "failed states," or the absence of governmental authority, a return to anarchy and lawlessness.

Chapter 2

Economic and financial crises are sobering events. They put people out of work, derailing lives and generating considerable social dislocation. They tend to have concentrated effects by industry and by location, oftentimes throwing entire communities into disarray, forcing young people to look for opportunities elsewhere, and contributing to urban decay and squalor. People who have worked for decades in a certain occupation find themselves left behind as jobs disappear and their chances of acquiring new skills dim.

One of the landmark achievements of the liberal order that emerged out of World War II had been to reduce the frequency of economic and financial crises to historic lows. During the 1950s and 1960s relatively few countries experienced major economic dislocations. Although the oil crises of the 1970s put stress on many economies, the number and frequency of crises did not reach historic highs until the 1980s and 1990s, mostly driven by the contagious effect of short-term capital flows. This type of footloose money would later play a crucial role in the global financial crisis. Unlike the investments made by companies in manufacturing plants, warehouses, sales subsidiaries, or other types of facilities, short-term money is not committed to a particular goal as it incessantly seeks the highest return, adjusted for risk.

Another critical fault line in the evolution of globalization has been the proliferation of failed states. When a state breaks down, there is lawlessness, chaos, anarchy. Somalia often comes to mind as the quintessential example of a country that descended into chaos, economic dislocation, poverty, and forced migration. The graphic image of pirates taking over merchant vessels is deeply ingrained in the minds of many people who perhaps do not realize that the impoverished communities along the Somali shores had suffered from years of environmental damage by the very ships that dumped all sorts of waste near the coast. Long-festering civil wars and the breakup of the Soviet Union into myriad independent countries increased the number of failed states. By 1995 researchers determined that seventy-eight countries in the world were failed states, a whopping 42 percent of the total. Civil war and state failure gave rise in some cases to organized groups such as the Islamic State in Iraq and Syria. Fortunately, that number came down steadily to fifty by 2015 as civil wars ended and state structures were rebuilt. The geography of state failure—affecting mostly Africa, the Middle East, and parts of South Asia—means that the world faces an enormous challenge. Those parts of the world are characterized by rapidly growing populations, high unemployment, poverty, corruption, and great natural wealth in the form of fossil fuels and strategic minerals. That is a notoriously unstable and explosive cocktail.

Globalization also contributed to a third phenomenon associated with uncertainty and chaos in the world, the declining quality of democratic practices. Democracy had been widely adopted as a form of government, but actual political practices differed greatly. More countries than ever managed to adopt a stable and well-functioning democratic framework of government, but many others called themselves democracies while in reality they were far from being so. In theory, they appeared to be democracies, but in practice they represented uneasy combinations of democratic and authoritarian traits. These "anocracies" were amalgams in which elections were regularly held, but in the absence of true multiparty competition and free, open political debate. Typically, an individual or group of individuals came to perpetuate themselves in power through covert coercion, manipulation of the media, and intimidation and incarceration of political opponents. Prominent examples of this pattern include Venezuela, Zimbabwe, Russia, and Turkey. The number of anocracies grew during the 1960s and 1970s as new countries became independent states, but tended to decline thereafter as many of them became stable democracies. However, the prevalence of this peculiar problem increased again during the 1990s with the end of the Cold War, and has not subsided since then. Roughly one in four countries in the world nowadays are anocracies, mostly situated in Latin America, Africa, the former Soviet Union, and the Middle East.

As if economic crises, failed states, and anocracies were not enough, the fourth element of instability that continued to undermine the Global Liberal Order is terrorism, a form of violent conflict that mutated during the 1990s and went viral after the 9/11 attacks. It is hardly an exaggeration to assert that terrorism has reshaped global politics, and that the very nature of the state has changed as a result, given the resources allocated to the military and to the security agencies in an effort to fight it. Terrorism strikes at the heart of the Global Liberal Order, instilling fears in the citizenry and prompting the leaders of democracies to curtail some individual freedoms on the justification that fighting it requires some tradeoffs and compromises. The free movement of people has come under attack, and the right to privacy has been undercut by antiterrorism policies. The debate over the best way to handle terrorism split public opinion into several factions, with one of them espousing xenophobic policies to bring this, as well as other problems, to an end. Terrorism has, in effect, contributed to the polarization of politics in both the United States and Europe. An especially problematic aspect of terrorism is that it is concentrated in a handful of unstable countries, including Iraq, Afghanistan, Pakistan, Nigeria, Syria, Russia, and India.

For its part, the global liberal economic order was already under stress for two structural reasons. One had to do with the fragmentation of geopolitical and economic power in the world, and the other with income and wealth inequality. Prior to 1989 the world of free markets and free polities had one uncontested leader, the United States. This state of affairs was challenged by the formation of the European Union in 1993, a bloc intended not only to facilitate economic activity and trade within its boundaries, but also to turn itself into an economic and technological powerhouse on a par with the United States in a world vastly redefined by the collapse of the Soviet Union. Soon thereafter, persistently high growth rates in emerging markets, especially China, Brazil, and India, made the world realize that in the near future most economic activity would unfold in a different part of the world than during the previous 250 years. By the early years of the twenty-first century, China had become the world's largest trading nation, and India had embarked on a high-growth path. The leader of the post–World War II Global Liberal Order was still the largest economy, the most technologically advanced, and the financial powerhouse. Within a decade or so, China will become the largest middle-class consumer market in the world, with India following suit perhaps two decades later. These seemingly great advantages represented weaknesses as well, as the crisis of 2008 would demonstrate.

The second structural change had been brewing since the 1970s, and had to do with the distribution of income and wealth. The backbone of the U.S. and European economies was the middle class. In fact, it was also the anchor of the political system. Parties and political candidates ran for office on policies mainly oriented toward the middle class. After two decades of income growth, it became increasingly difficult for the average citizen to see a future in which his or her economic status would be better than that of the previous generation. Free trade and capital flows undermined the manufacturing economies of the richest countries, with many jobs moving offshore. Most importantly, however, technology created amazing opportunities for many while at the same time threatening entire occupations and making it possible to produce more with less, both in the manufacturing and in the service sector. As incomes stagnated, the European and American middle class saw almost no increase in its standard of living. Meanwhile, poverty increased and a greater percentage of wealth came to be enjoyed by those at the top. While the segment of the rich grew very fast in the emerging markets, they also witnessed a rapid expansion of the middle class, with hundreds of millions of people being raised into it across the globe by the rising tide of economic growth. Young people in China or India saw new horizons ahead of them, while those in Europe and the United States felt crushed. The decline of the middle class in Europe and the United States was compounded in its effects by the crisis of 2008.

The Crisis of 2008

In the midst of the cross-currents caused by failed states, authoritarian democracies (or anocracies), the growing importance of the emerging economies, and rising inequality, the global economy came to the brink of collapse in 2008 after the implosion of U.S. financial markets. Starting as a meltdown of the housing market and securitized mortgage loans, it quickly spread to the entire financial system and ultimately to the real economy not only in the United States but also in Europe and elsewhere. Emerging markets weathered the storm relatively well, but it took major interventions by the Federal Reserve and other central banks to prevent the entire global economy from collapsing.

The crisis had two important effects. One was to cast doubt on the liberal model of the market economy, especially in its financial aspects, and the other was to accelerate the trend toward a multipolar world in which emerging economies would play a pivotal role. In addition, it marked the beginning of Russian efforts to discredit the Western democracies. Liberal economic thought was based on the fundamental assumption that markets are self-correcting. The crisis of 2008 demonstrated that the pursuit of self-interest did not necessarily translate into economic well-being for everyone. Moreover, the financial collapse exposed greed as rampant behavior among market participants. People who felt left behind witnessed in disbelief how bankers and money managers got away with exposing their own companies and the entire financial system to inordinate levels of risk. Never in recent economic history had so few harmed so many to such an extent, with impunity. Meanwhile, many people lost their homes, their savings, and their jobs.

The crisis exposed some important cracks in Version 2.0 of the Global Liberal Order. First and foremost, it demonstrated that financial liberalization had gone too far. Financial institutions, especially investment banks, used leverage and multiple subterfuges to maximize returns. Meanwhile, the regulatory and supervisory structures and agencies inherited from the Great Depression were not overhauled, updated, and empowered to keep a close watch on the new large, complex, and diversified financial institutions that emerged from deregulation and liberalization during the 1990s. Market participants launched new products linked to highly cyclical assets such as those in the housing sector, with little or no sense as to how they might be affected by a recession. Fancy mathematical formulas and financial theories came in handy to justify the new, profitable field of derivatives. Too many individuals and financial companies believed that the system was safe. A large number understood that things might go wrong, but they could not or did not want to switch gears before the implosion. A not insignificant number expected that they would be rescued if it came to that. Many of the banks had become "too big to fail," and thus eligible for a government bailout. Clearly, if markets had ever been capable of anticipating problems, they did not in the years leading up to 2008.

While the crisis did not create income and wealth inequality from scratch, it did exacerbate a process that had taken a turn for the worse since the 1970s in both the United States and Europe. Between the mid-1990s and the mid-2000s inequality within countries increased in most, with the notable exceptions of Brazil, Russia, Mexico,

Nigeria, Turkey, and Spain. Most importantly, in the two most populous countries, China and India, there has been a sharp increase in inequality. Data for China indicate that most of the increase is attributable to yawning disparities within urban areas, and between rural and urban areas. Inequality in rural areas has remained constant or decreased slightly. For India, no national index exists, but we also observe over time growing income inequality within cities, and between cities and the countryside. Thus, the increase in inequality within the two countries with the largest populations as well as several developed ones (e.g., Germany, Sweden, and the United States) overshadows the decrease in other, smaller countries. Much of the widening income gap has to do with stagnating wages, which represent 75 percent of household income.[1]

Inequality has risen even in countries traditionally thought to be egalitarian, like Germany, Denmark, and Sweden, where the top 10 percent now receives five times as much income as the bottom 10 percent. In many advanced economies the multiple has reached 10 (e.g., Italy, Japan, Korea, and the United Kingdom), and even 14 (Israel and the United States). Latin America stands out as an especially unequal part of the world. In Chile and Mexico the multiple is 25, and in Brazil as high as 50. Among OECD countries, the multiple has grown from the mid-1980s to the late 2000s in Australia, Austria, Canada, Czech Republic, Denmark, Finland, Germany Hungary, Israel, Luxembourg, Mexico, the Netherlands, New Zealand, Norway, Sweden, the United Kingdom, and the United States.

Inequality, of course, is a multidimensional problem. Most studies find that wealth inequality is even greater than income inequality, and that it is on the increase within countries as well. While in 2000 the top 10 percent of households in the world owned 85 percent of the wealth, they accounted for 67 percent of the income. At the present time the wealth of the top 1 percent in the world is greater than the wealth of the rest of us. Across countries, we observe a decrease in inequality in terms of education, knowledge, and other human development variables, except for life expectancy, due mostly to the impact of the AIDS epidemic in sub-Saharan Africa.[2]

Increasing unequal income and wealth distributions are not only socially undesirable but also a potential brake on economic growth and a factor that can fuel financial crises. Western economies were essentially driven by consumer spending. The hollowing out of the middle class posed a serious threat to economic growth. In fact, the average post–World War II recession in the United States lasted less than four quarters. The Great Recession of 2007–2009 was the longest lasting since the Great Depression of the 1930s. In Europe it took even longer for the economy to recover, especially because many countries went through a horrible "double-dip" recession. Thus, inequality was in part driven by the dynamics set into motion by Version 2.0 of the Global Liberal Order. It also became its biggest threat, undermining the public's confidence in the free market.

Chapter 3

New Actors Enter the Stage

In the wake of the crisis, reasons for the undoing of the Global Liberal Order Version 2.0 became the subject of heated debates in the media, at international summits, in government circles, and among ordinary citizens. One must start by recognizing the limitations, and in some cases petty attitudes, of the architects and the builders of the Global Liberal Order and of those opposing it. The roots of the crisis of economic liberalism lie in overly optimistic views about the role of knowledge, science, and the kinds of incentives that elicit the type of behavior that propels economies toward growth.

Dogmatism and Intransigence

One of the key contributions of liberalism was an openness of mind and spirit that stood in sharp contrast to the obscurantism and dogmatism of other ways of thinking about how to organize society and the economy. It is nearly impossible to understand why, in the face of mounting challenges, liberal economic and political elites turned enthusiastically technocratic sometime during the 1980s. In the wake of declining performance, technocrats stuck to their guns, claiming that the economy was not doing well because their designs were not being implemented correctly. Eventually, this type of argument alienated voters, who turned against the technocrats at elections in Britain, the United States, and several European countries during the 2010s.

Technocracy literally means rule by those who bring technical expertise to governing. In its modern manifestation, technocracy is based on the basic notion that social and economic problems can be framed in scientific terms with the aim of finding a solution to them. Not everyone has expertise to frame problems in this fashion; only the technocrats. Thus, decision making concerning complex problems should be left to them. Most importantly, technocrats believe that the role of politics should be minimal, and that political "interference" will almost surely lead to suboptimal results.

Technocrats managed to gain a stronghold in certain types of institutions during the 1980s and 1990s. First they colonized think tanks and other similar research-oriented institutions. Then they persuaded governments in as many as eighty countries around the world that it was important to have a central bank independent from the political power so that it could have a free hand to combat inflation, which was constructed as the leading economic problem at the time. Most importantly, they took the helm of key international agencies such as the World Bank, the Bank for International Settlements, and the International Monetary Fund (IMF). The tide of technocratic thinking and practice took over the global economy and parts of the state.[1]

Some of the most momentous technocratic decisions, with large implications for the future, were made at the IMF by a cadre of economists led by French technocrat Michel Camdessus. Between 1995 and 1999, this group dealt with the crises in Latin America, East Asia, and Russia by emphasizing not only macroeconomic adjustment but also institutional reforms, in what became to be known as the "expanded Washington Consensus." Loans to economies in disarray were made conditional on specific reforms regarding trade, taxes, spending, labor market regulations, and corporate governance rules, among many others. For instance, the conditional loan program for Indonesia in 1998 included a record 140 clauses demanding specific reforms in exchange for money.

Not surprisingly, emerging economies responded to these technocratic requirements with disbelief. However, they had no option but to comply, at least in the short term. One especially important development was China's reaction. Although the country did not need IMF assistance at the time, its leaders vowed to accumulate enough reserves to make any such intervention unnecessary in the future. China's quest for a large current account surplus to build up its reserves would change the global economy forever.

The accumulation of foreign-exchange reserves by emerging economies posed a peculiar challenge for the post–World War II Global Liberal Order. In 2005, the amount of reserves held by emerging economies surpassed the amount held by developed countries for the first time in history. By 2016 the reserves were twice as large. Meanwhile, about 55 percent of the voting power at the IMF was still held by the developed countries. The other 45 percent was so thinly spread around the emerging and developing world that the growing power of the largest Asian economies was not well reflected. As of 2017 China had a voting quota of 6.09 percent, and India a mere 2.64 percent, compared to 3.02 percent for Italy, 4.03 percent each for France and the United Kingdom, 5.32 percent for Germany, 6.15 percent for Japan, and 16.52 percent for the United States.

Political Opportunism, Nationalism, and Populism

Technological change, inequality, and the alleged negative impact of free trade are fertile soil for political entrepreneurs. When, in the wake of so much change and upheaval, the electorate naturally turns desperate for new approaches, opportunists such as Farage, Le Pen, Wilders, or Trump emerge. It is also a situation in which old-school autocratic populists like Putin, Maduro, or Duterte may thrive. Can the Global Liberal Order survive such formidable enemies?

There are two essential features to populist politics. The first is the tendency to frame the situation in simplistic ways that lead to seemingly straightforward analyses of the problems confronting society or the economy. Typically, such "analyses" end up blaming very specific forces or agents for the problems. The second ingredient is to propose overly simplistic solutions to the problems identified as such, frequently proposing a magic bullet that would help overcome them. A related aspect of populism is the absence of a debate about the true costs of the proposed solutions, and of the tradeoffs involved. Most of the time, populists underestimate the budgetary impact of their proposals. In-depth discussion or debates of how problems are framed and solutions are devised is not a priority for populists. In fact, they tend to distrust and seek to undermine the institutions that are supposed to foster such debates, including parliament, the judiciary, the media, think tanks, and universities, among others. In some cases, populist politicians seek to hijack the state to create a clientelistic ecosystem. Populism is essentially antielitist, and suspicious and resentful of technocratic approaches.[2] While it supports majority rule, it deviates sharply from liberal democracy in that it recognizes and respects no institutional checks and balances. It proposes a direct relationship between the leader and the led.

Sometimes populism comes together joined with nationalism. Nations are socially constructed entities in that they are "imagined because the members of even the smallest nation will never know most of their fellow-members, meet them, or even hear of them, yet in the minds of each lives the image of their communion."[3] *Nationalism* refers to beliefs and efforts advocating for the establishment or the improvement of a nation. Nationalist policies are those geared toward the strengthening of the feeling or the reality of nationhood. Oftentimes the process of nation building coincides with that of state building, culminating in the formation of a nation-state. The Global Liberal Order depends crucially on the international system of nation-states, given that it was created and continues to be supported by nation-states agreeing to liberal principles of economic and political organization. Needless to say, there are quite a few plurinational states in the world as well as stateless nations.

In the economic sphere, however, nationalist policies are frequently associated with trade protectionism, capital controls, immigration restrictions, and other similar measures that shelter domestic markets for goods, services, capital, and labor from foreign competition. In the political realm, the term *nativism* is sometimes used to refer to right-wing versions of nationalism that incorporate xenophobic ideas.[4] Economic nationalism is sometimes geared toward helping domestic industry gain experience and scale before exposing it to the rigors of international competition. That was the policy implemented during certain time periods by many successful countries, including Germany, the United States, Japan, and South Korea. The problem is that this so-called infant-industry protectionism can lead to stagnation if domestic interest groups become entrenched and lobby for the continuation of protectionism, as happened in Latin America during the 1960s and 1970s.

Nationalist-populist policies are especially noteworthy because they combine the worst of both concepts, namely, an emotional prioritization of a nation's own well-being at the expense of everyone else's, and a systematic oversimplification of both problems and solutions. Common to most strands of the populist rhetoric and nationalist narratives alike is the victimization of the people and the demonization of the agents allegedly responsible for the ills that lie at the heart of their grievances. The people, normally though not always a nation, are presented as the victim of mistaken or ill-conceived domestic or foreign policies. Neutralizing or deflecting the agents who caused harm represents the ultimate goal of populist and nationalist arguments and actions. Given these features, it should be no surprise that, most of the time, the nationalist, populist, or nationalist-populist politicians that succeed in reaching power or being influential tend to behave opportunistically, i.e., they exploit specific circumstances and moments to make general claims about the best political and economic course of action and to advance their desire to rule. They exploit economic and cultural grievances among the public ruthlessly, and with little if any commitment to actually improving their lot.

Nationalist-populist narratives come in two broad kinds. There is a right-wing nationalist-populist rhetoric that emphasizes the allegedly disastrous effects of immigration and the loss of sovereignty brought about by free trade and free capital flows, let alone monetary union with other countries. And there is a left-wing nationalist-populist rhetoric that highlights the catastrophic effects of free trade and free capital flows on the labor market, and espouses some reservations and misgivings about technological change. Note that, while both detest free trade and free capital flows, they do so for different reasons. Both exhibit a contempt toward technocrats, professional politicians, and the so-called deep state, that is, the civil servants and career bureaucrats whose role is to use applied knowledge to tackle practical policy problems. Thus, much of the liberal agenda has recently come under the cross-fire of attacks from the Right and the Left.

To summarize, the nationalist-populist rhetoric starts by decrying the decay of the nation, its betrayal by economic, financial, political, and cultural elites (including the media), those who profit from open borders and inflows of foreign goods and immigrants. The proposed solution is to again put the nation first (especially ahead of the individual), to build walls, to cleanse the nation of outside influences and from outsiders, to regenerate the body politic ("drain the swamp"), and return to the true essence of the nation in a catharsis of sorts. National-populism thrives when the market economy does not perform well or goes through a crisis, when economic inequality increases, when the middle class feels squeezed, and when liberal democracy is perceived as failing the people.

One final tendency among nationalist-populist movements is the yearning for a leader, and the elevation of that person above whatever his or her proposals might be. In other words, the leader becomes more important than the actual policies. Not all nationalist-populist political movements share this feature. One can find many that do, both on the right and the left. This is certainly the case with Maduro, Erdogan, and Putin. A cult of personality also played a role in Italy and the United States with Berlusconi and Trump. In both cases, business acumen and allegedly demonstrated success in business are used to rally the base of disgruntled supporters to the cause of making the government work for the people by removing incompetent politicians. Trump also sought to weaken the layer of career bureaucrats and technocrats separating him from the people and from international leaders, thus fostering a direct rapprochement with them. Distrust, or open hostility, toward this deep state has become a trademark of populist and nationalist politicians in the United States and Europe.

Interestingly, among scholars and members of the establishment, the terms *nationalist* and *populist* have utterly negative connotations. Not so among the people who support and vote for nationalist and populist candidates. They reframe the term *nationalism* as patriotism, and the nation as a safe haven that protects them from unwanted foreign influences. And they reinterpret the term *populism* as the political and policy manifestation of the will of the people. In so doing, supporters provide a formidable rationale for pursuing nationalist-populist proposals at a time when so many feel betrayed by the elites. This type of nationalist-populist rhetoric has prospered both on the right and the left, achieving levels of legitimacy and parliamentary representation unheard of during the post–World War II decades.

The Far Right in Europe

Over the last fifteen years Far Right nationalist-populist parties have grown considerably in their electoral appeal throughout Europe, posing a major challenge to the Global Liberal Order, both politically and economically. In terms of popular support, the ranking as of 2017 from more to less support was as follows: Hungary, Poland, Switzerland, Austria, France, Belgium, Denmark, Finland, Bulgaria, Greece, the Netherlands, Italy, Slovakia, the Czech Republic, Sweden, the United Kingdom, Romania, and Germany. Among major countries, only Ireland, Portugal, and Spain proved immune to this trend. Romanians' support for such parties at the polls ended in 2012.[5] Thus, it is breathtaking to realize that the geography of right-wing nationalist-populism in Europe extends five thousand miles from the Arctic Circle to the Mediterranean, and a similar distance from the Irish Sea to the Black Sea. Sociodemographically, the most reliable supporters of the Far Right tend to be male, with no college education, and above the age of fifty. This demographic group has become pivotal when it comes to deciding electoral outcomes on both sides of the Atlantic. It is, by a wide margin, the group most severely affected by technological change and free trade. It is the key constituency that propelled Trump to victory.

While Far Right parties have failed to gain a majority, or even a plurality, of the vote in national elections, they have participated in coalition governments in Austria, Croatia, Estonia, Finland, Italy, Latvia, the Netherlands, Poland, Serbia, Slovakia, and Switzerland, and they have supported minority governments in Bulgaria, Denmark, the Netherlands, and Norway.[6] Thus, their influence has already been felt in the actual workings of policy making. From this point of view, Europe today looks vastly different from the Europe of the 1990s. At the very least, the rise of the Far Right has forced the established parties to either double down on their principles and beliefs, or to incorporate selective aspects of the radicals' proposals. It has changed the political landscape, even if radicals do not achieve a working majority in the future. They have redefined the boundaries of acceptable political discourse, and they have forced other political movements and parties to recalibrate their approaches.

Some of the most extreme right-wing nationalist-populist parties are to be found in countries that most observers would identify as being close to the model of the ideal liberal democracy. Thus, the Party for Freedom in the Netherlands finished second in the March 15, 2017, parliamentary election, winning five additional seats for a total of twenty out of 150. Its leader, Geert Wilders, employs fiery anti-Islamic rhetoric and is against the European Union. Another right-wing party, the Forum for Democracy, won two seats.

In Austria, a country with a more complex historical legacy, Norbert Hofer of the Freedom Party was the frontrunner in the first round of the 2017 presidential election, losing in the runoff with 49.7 percent of the vote. After the High Court ordered a repeat of the election, about 6 percent of the voters defected from him.

In Greece the Golden Dawn party has had a parliamentary presence for years. This quasi-fascist—sometimes called neo-Nazi—movement is anti-EU, anti-euro, anti-immigrant, and pro-Russia. It has been upstaged by Syriza, a left-wing nationalist-populist party that has governed Greece almost continuously since 2015. Still, Golden Dawn stunned everyone in 2012 by receiving nearly 7 percent of the vote and gaining 21 parliamentary seats out of 300. "The Golden Dawn is an ultranationalist group that emphasizes the superiority of Greek lineage, Greece's unique language and ancient heritage." They believe that the "Greek nation is under threat and constantly undergoing an ideological battle to be salvaged from destruction. But what makes the Golden Dawn a fascist formation, rather than a patriotic or nationalist group, is not simply its ultra-nationalism, [. . .] but more specifically the theme of palingenesis—the key theme of national rebirth which forms the Golden Dawn's 'nationalist solution' to social decadence."[7]

France is another country with a long and difficult history of flirtation with Far Right proposals, especially during the Nazi occupation and then again with the Algerian War. The Front National has come to attract 25 to 30 percent of the vote, although its parliamentary presence is much smaller due to the allocation of seats under existing electoral rules. In 2002 the party's founder, Jean-Marie Le Pen, competed in the run-off presidential election after finishing ahead of the Socialist candidate in the first round. His daughter Marine Le Pen repeated the same feat in the

2017 election. At the local level, the National Front came to control several second-tier municipalities after the 2014 election. That same year it became the largest French delegation to the European Parliament, after winning a stunning 25 percent of the vote. The Front National defends anti-EU and anti-immigrant policies, and has benefited from the rise of radical Islamic terrorism in France. Men with no college education and Roman Catholics are more likely to support the Front National. Geographically, most of its support comes from the economically depressed northeast of France, and the Mediterranean coast, where, in addition to relatively high unemployment, most of the 1.5 million French returnees from Algeria live along with their descendants.

The origins of the Front National go back to the Ordre Nouveau, a neofascist movement intended to unify the French Far Right during the 1950s and 1960s. Its ideology was vehemently antiliberal, anticapitalist, and anti-Marxist. It was in many ways a radical Catholic and ultraconservative movement. Jean-Marie Le Pen was chosen as the leader in the 1970s because he was relatively moderate. It was easy for opponents on the moderate right to claim that the Front National did not stand by the cherished principles of laicism and republicanism. Marine Le Pen's strategy was to modernize the discourse by turning it on its head. She claimed that the Front National was the only party that defended the true essence of the republic by attacking immigration and proposing to extricate France from the shackles of the European Union. Presidents Mitterrand and Sarkozy helped the Front National become a legitimate political force. Mitterrand encouraged the growth of the Front National in order to divide the Right, and Sarkozy incorporated into his discourse many aspects of the Front National's platform, thus legitimizing it. Consequently, the Front National made the transition from an antisystem party to an antiestablishment party, inviting increasing numbers of French voters to reject the traditional political parties for not putting France first. The media also played into its hands by labeling it as a "populist" party, thus relegating the harsher and more stigmatizing "extreme Right" designation to the background. Unlike French elites, many people came to view this populist party as one whose goal was to further the wish of the people as opposed to an authoritarian or neofascist political movement. The Front National "managed through its counter-hegemonic strategy to fill a void in French liberal democracy created by the apparent powerlessness of mainstream parties to offer anything meaningful to an increasingly disillusioned and distrustful electorate."[8]

The largest Eastern European economy, Poland, is the country that has fallen for the Far Right most decisively. The Law and Justice Party, led by Jaroslaw Kaccynski, won the parliamentary elections of 2015 with 39 percent of the vote. The government has since restricted political freedoms, limited the power of the courts, and tightened its grip over the media. In July 2017 President Trump visited the country and praised its government. In Hungary, the Fidesz Party led by Viktor Orban has run on a joint list with the KDNP, a Christian Democratic party, and won the last two parliamentary elections. Increasingly aligned with Putin, the Hungarian right wing has succeeded at implementing anti-immigrant policies.

Also in Hungary, the racist Jobbik party has gained notoriety by focusing its attacks on the Roma minority, abandoning its early anti-Semitic rhetoric. In the 2009 European Parliament election they received 8 percent of the vote, in the 2010 Hungarian parliamentary election just above 16 percent, and in the 2014 Hungarian parliamentary election a whopping 20 percent. "Jobbik was unique among European radicals in being pro-Muslim, which can be explained either by ideological reasons based on a pan-Turanian [i.e., pan-Turkist] vision and an anti-Semitic logic [. . .] or by financial reasons for the alleged secret financial support from Iran and Syria."[9]

Perhaps the most incomprehensible of all is the rise of the Far Right in Scandinavia, once the champion of "capitalism with a human face" and home to some of the most extensive welfare states in the world. The Sweden Democrats won 49 seats in the 439-seat lower chamber with 13 percent of the vote. In Denmark, the already Far Right Danish People's Party, which commanded 21 percent of the vote in the 2015 election, was challenged further to the right by the New Right, which will participate for the first time in the 2019 election. In Finland, the Finns Party won 19 percent of the vote in the 2011 parliamentary election, finishing third. In 2015 it finished second in a more fragmented election with nearly 18 percent. As a result, the Finns Party joined the governing coalition.

In Scandinavia, the growth of the Far Right quickened when segments of the population adopted an ethnic-based concept of the nation under the perceived threat of immigration. This was especially the case in Sweden, a country with high immigration and refugee inflows. "Those voting for the Sweden Democrats were much more likely to have a thicker, exclusionary conception of national identity than voters for other parties. [. . .] Talking about national identity per se may not increase hostility. Instead it matters hugely *how* we talk about national identity and who belongs to the nation."[10]

Europe's economic and financial powerhouse is not immune to right-wing extremism either, in spite of Franz-Josef Strauss's dictum that "there is nothing to the right of the CSU [Christian-Social Union] but a wall."[11] Alternative for Germany came into being in 2012 as an anti-euro movement and party. The party did not manage to gain parliamentary representation in 2013 because of the restrictive 5-percent rule, which it narrowly missed, but it attracted as much as 25 percent of the vote in some regional elections in 2016. In the September 2017 election it easily gained parliamentary representation with 13 percent of the vote, becoming the third political force with 95 seats. Alternative for Germany has its origins in racist theories about the potential disintegration of Germany under high levels of immigration. But the party was also elitist and opposed social programs for the disadvantaged, even if they were Germans. The bailout of the Greek economy represented a catalyzing event because many Germans believed Greece should have been left to its fate.

The most radical political movement against immigration, and especially refugees, is Pegida, Patriotic Europeans against the Islamization of the Western World, which successfully staged weekly demonstrations with tens of thousands of people, especially in eastern German cities. As in France, Alternative for Germany and Pegida accuse the government of betraying the nation with its pro-immigration and pro-European policies. Pegida's frequent attacks on refugees and their accommodations caused Alternative for Germany to distance itself.

It seems clear that the strong showings of the Far Right throughout most of Europe will continue for the foreseeable future. Continued immigration, frequent terrorist attacks, political corruption, population ageing, institutional crises in the European Union, and/or persistently high unemployment provide right-wing nationalist-populist politicians with ample opportunities to persuade a sizable chunk of the electorate to vote for them. In a continent that is rapidly aging and losing competitiveness, the liberal message has lost some of its appeal.

The most puzzling absence of a Far Right xenophobic party is in Spain. This is a country in which the immigrant population grew rapidly from 3 percent of the total in 1998 to 13 percent in 2008. The impact of the crisis was intense, with unemployment exceeding 20 percent for several years, and rising inequality. By 2014 Spain ranked as the country in Europe with the widest gap between the top 10 percent and the bottom 10 percent in the income distribution. Corruption cases afflicted both the conservative and socialist parties, the two dominant political forces. Moreover, both the socialist and conservative governments responded to the crisis by implementing austerity policies, with the corresponding budget cuts. Two new parties emerged, one at the center of the political spectrum, between the conservatives and the socialists (Ciudadanos), and the other to the left of the socialists (Podemos). But why did no party emerge to the Far Right?[12]

The transition to democracy in Spain and the new model of territorial administration deemphasized appeals to Spanish nationalism, mostly as a reaction against the nearly four decades of Franco's dictatorship, thus favoring the emergence and consolidation of alternative identities in the various parts of the country. In the historic cases of Basque and Catalan nationalism, each with their own language, institutions, and culture, the nationalist political parties on the right won most elections, with a message of moderation and a firm commitment to free markets and to European integration. In fact, Spaniards are more pro-European than typically found in the EU. "This Europeanism presents itself not only as a cultural identification with Europe, but also as sympathy with the EU as a political project."[13] Another big difference is that there was little criticism of globalization or trade, even during the crisis. Attitudes toward immigration were the most tolerant in the EU, although they had become closer to the mean by 2007. Anti-immigrant sentiment peaked in 2011–2012, and started to decline as many foreign-born workers returned home after losing their jobs, especially in the construction sector. In spite of the March 2004 terrorist attack in Madrid, which claimed 190 lives, most people do not hold anti-Muslim views.

The combination of relatively mild anti-immigrant feelings and weak national identification made it hard for a strong Far Right party to emerge in Spain. In addition, civil society rushed to help immigrant groups through the establishment of myriad nongovernmental organizations. Moreover, the Catholic Church saw in immigration, especially from Latin America, an opportunity to spread its charitable message and to expand its reach in a country that had gone through a very rapid process of secularization. These factors meant that during the early years after the reestablishment of democracy, the Far Right never obtained more than 2 percent of the vote, winning at most one seat in parliament. The conservative and religious vote went to the conservative Popular Party, which espoused relatively moderate views and managed to attract to its orbit most of the people who felt nostalgic about the Franco years.[14]

The case of Spain suggests that the Far Right does not get that far in elections without strong nationalist sentiments among the people. The absence of nationalism makes it impossible to argue that foreign forces are undermining the health of the nation and threatening its existence. As a result, the message of xenophobia has little traction.

The Radical Left, also in Europe

While the traditional moderate Left (i.e., Social Democratic) and Far Left (Communist) parties in Western Europe continue to decline, a new breed of left-wing political movements has come of age. They espouse populist policies, with few or no nationalist ideas. The key differences between right-wing and left-wing populism has to do with the former's acceptance of the market economy and the latter's rejection of anti-immigrant attitudes and policies and antisystem and antimarket views. Still, the two agree on the need for trade protections and tighter regulation of the financial sector. Many Far Left parties argue for nationalization of banks, utilities, and other large companies in strategic sectors.

Greece and Spain are the posterchildren of the alternative Left and its capacity to mobilize support among those negatively affected by the crisis. Syriza, a coalition of left-wing parties that came to power on an antiausterity platform, has gained the support of slightly more than a third of the electorate. Its leader, Alexis Tsipras, has been the country's prime minister since 2015. While he has worked to soften the austerity policies imposed by the troika of the European Union, European Central Bank, and IMF, unemployment remained above 20 percent, with the economy's growth rate below 1 percent, and social problems continue to mount.

The rise of Podemos in Spain was equally meteoric, although it failed to dislodge the Socialist Party from leading the Left or the conservative Popular Party from power. The fact that Podemos has hit an electoral ceiling is surprising given the myriad corruption scandals that have afflicted the two largest parties. Podemos or its local allies did win in municipal elections, gaining control over some of the country's largest cities, including Madrid and Barcelona. While controversial in some respects, the policies implemented by Podemos mayors in these cities have been well received by a significant proportion of the population, especially those limiting gentrification and enhancing social services.

Both Syriza and Podemos are highly suspicious of, if not flatly opposed to, various aspects of the Global Liberal Order, especially Version 2.0. Chief among their beliefs is that free trade and free capital movements have benefited the few at the expense of the many.[15] This is a complex issue that we will analyze below.

The British Debacle

While the crisis made the Euro Zone countries miserable for lack of exchange-rate flexibility, the British economy did relatively well between 2010 and 2016. It presented itself to the world as a thriving country committed to liberal political and economic values, with the ability to attract talent and the determination to chart its own course of action within the European Union. To be sure, the old divisions between the rural areas and the big cities and between southeastern England and the rest of the country continued unabated, but nothing on the horizon signaled a major disruption.

The prime minister at the time was David Cameron, who was growing increasingly impatient with two unresolved issues in British politics. The first was the possibility of Scottish independence, and the second the complaints within his own party about the erosion of British sovereignty as a result of EU-level legislation and policies. Known as a risk taker, Cameron decided to settle, at least for the next generation, the Scottish question. He succeeded at winning in a referendum in spite of the terrible campaign of the "remainer" camp. In fact, much credit went to the last-minute emotional and widely seen televised speech by former prime minister Gordon Brown, a Labour politician from Scotland with impeccable credentials as a defender of the Global Liberal Order Version 2.0, as he demonstrated during his many years as chancellor of the exchequer under Tony Blair as prime minister. The main lesson from the Scottish referendum was that at least a subset of British voters was in no mood for a radical departure from the status quo.

Emboldened by this win, Cameron decided to put to rest the European question within his own party. If Scottish independence would have generated significant risks for both Scotland and the rest of the United Kingdom, Brexit certainly amounted to the equivalent of a geopolitical tectonic shift. After more than forty years of membership, the British economy and legal system were intricately intertwined with those of the rest of Europe. It was almost unthinkable that a majority of the British people would vote to undo so much history. Cameron appeared to think that the anti-European faction in his own party would be silenced by a resounding victory in a referendum. After all, Britain had already staged one referendum on continued membership in 1975, two years after the country became part of the bloc. That time it was a conservative government that had negotiated entry, and the Labour Party that included a referendum on its electoral platform. Upon winning the 1974 general election, Labour prime minister Harold Wilson called for a referendum, in which the option for continued membership won by a 2-to-1 margin. Interestingly, in this first referendum support for the remain camp was higher in most parts of England and Wales than in Scotland and Northern Ireland. Even more tellingly, opposition leader Margaret Thatcher campaigned for the yes vote. As in the 2016 referendum, the Labour leadership was divided between those actively in favor of membership and those skeptical of though not opposed to it. The EU evoked in the minds of Labour leaders and voters two opposed images. On the one hand, it stood for solidarity and the welfare state, but on the other it was associated with technocracy and austerity policies.

In 2016 the Labour Party was led by an old-school socialist, Jeremy Corbyn, who was not just skeptical but deeply concerned about the technocratic modus operandi at the EU and the austerity policies promoted by Brussels. He did practically nothing to mobilize the Labour vote in favor of continued membership. In addition, the overconfidence or hubris of the remain camp meant that the initiative was quickly seized by the leave camp, led not by dissenting tory backbenchers but by Nigel Farage, the leader of the UK Independence Party (UKIP), a peculiar political formation. Economically, the UKIP was neither populist nor nationalist in the sense that it did not promote clientelistic policies or protectionism. In fact, it was quite liberal in its economic arguments. Politically, it was staunchly nationalistic in that it yearned for a unitary British identity and advocated for less immigration. Its logo is fittingly a variation on the sign for the British pound. It was fundamentally a Eurosceptic party. One might argue that its very reason for existence was to unshackle Britain from the constraints of the EU.

It is possible that Cameron felt compelled to organize the Brexit referendum in order to prevent UKIP from gaining support among conservatives dissatisfied with his policies, especially those promulgated during the Conservative-Liberal Democrat coalition government. Farage once disparagingly accused Cameron of being "a socialist" whose priorities were "gay marriage, foreign aid, and wind farms."[16] In the 2014 election to the European Parliament, UKIP was the most voted party with 27.5 percent of the total, sending 24 members to Strasbourg, after capitalizing on its newly acquired appeal among traditional Labour voters in Wales and Northern England. It should be noted, however, that voters across Europe tend to use elections to the European Parliament to express their anger at politicians by voting for extreme options.

On the day of the Brexit referendum the exit polls and early returns indicated a very close outcome. By the early hours of the following morning the leave option was declared as the winner by 3.5 percentage points, with a 72 percent turnout. This meant that about 37 percent of all eligible voters went to the polls to reject membership in the EU. Cameron lasted less than a month as prime minister.

After a brief internal battle, Theresa May became the leader of the Conservative Party and the prime minister. May had little prior experience with European or economic affairs. In spite of having campaigned in favor of remaining, as prime minister she adopted a fairly hard line toward the coming Brexit negotiations with the EU. After formally initiating the two-year process of leaving the bloc, May sought to consolidate her leadership within her party and to amass a solid majority in parliament by calling for an early election in June 2017.

During the campaign, May failed to inspire and to reassure. By contrast, Corbyn managed to do both. May's strategy was to argue that Britain would be better off with a strong government negotiating favorable terms of Brexit. She seemed to ignore the well-documented fact that voters tend to be suspicious about early elections, especially at a time when many people were questioning again the arguments for leaving. Most fundamentally, the May campaign forgot that the Brexit vote was not about the ills of the EU but a protest vote against economic inequality and stagnation among certain segments of the population. Corbyn managed to focus the attention on the problems of ordinary people. When all the votes were counted, the conservatives had lost their majority, forcing them to enter into negotiations with Northern Ireland's Democratic Unionist Party to form a minority government. Meanwhile the Labour Party gained thirty seats. Interestingly, UKIP ended up empty handed, and the Scottish National

Party lost twenty-one seats, thus reducing the chances of a future replay of the independence referendum.

Disconnecting the United Kingdom from the EU may turn into a nightmare. Tens of thousands of British laws may have to be revised given that they were issued to conform to EU directives. Europe is the most important market for UK exports. A sudden Brexit would leave in limbo about 1.2 million British citizens who live in other EU countries as well as the 3 million EU citizens who live in the United Kingdom. It is in the British national interest to continue collaboration on topics as diverse as counterterrorism, international policing, national defense, climate change, and UN-sponsored missions, topics that the United Kingdom and the rest of Europe tend to agree on. Even more fundamentally, Britain is interested in preserving the Global Liberal Order, especially Version 2.0, given its economy's focus on financial services. Under German leadership, the EU is also committed to it.

The election of Emmanuel Macron as president of France in May 2017 dissipates an important doubt about the future of the EU. Germany and France are likely to once again become the dual engine of European integration. Britain has never quite fit in the Franco-German worldview. While Brexit will be strenuous on both sides, it does offer European leaders an opportunity to regroup and press ahead with their own agenda, now focused on making the single currency work for everyone and returning to economic growth. If Brexit takes place, Britain will need to reinvent itself in a major way. It has the Global Liberal Order Version 2.0 on its side. It just needs China and Germany to succeed at their efforts to preserve it. Or they need the new administration in the United States to fail at undermining it.

America Is No Exception: Trump as the Anti-Truman

In more ways than one, Donald Trump's electoral victory places the United States at the forefront of the antiliberal movement in the world. The new administration is certainly nationalistic in its framing of the major geopolitical and geoeconomic issues of the day. It is also populist in that it frames issues in oversimplified ways and offers simplistic solutions to them. As a candidate and president, Trump appealed to the anti-immigrant and isolationist undercurrents in American politics. He managed to put together an Electoral College majority on the basis of a veritable potpourri of voters, including most social conservatives, mainstream rural populations, a majority of people above the age of forty-five, a majority of those without a college degree, a majority of disgruntled blue-collar workers, a majority of white women and white men, and a third of Latinos/as.[17] He promised real walls, and as president built policy walls that isolate the United States from the rest of the world, walls that make the United States oblivious to the pressing issues facing humanity, from the refugee crisis to climate change, from growing inequality to discrimination against women and minorities, and from economic cooperation to global security, all the while diminishing the role of the United States in the world. He certainly is the anti-Truman.

At the 2017 annual meeting of the G20, Trump insisted on his "America first" policy. The other nineteen members reiterated in a communiqué their commitment to the Paris climate change accord. In separate bilateral talks, Trump predicted a quick trade deal with the United Kingdom and vowed that the wall at the U.S.-Mexican border would be built and that Mexico would pay for it. In a historic bilateral meeting, Russian president Vladimir Putin repeatedly denied any involvement in the U.S. election, contrary to the statements by the heads of the FBI, CIA, and the NSA, among other security agencies. Suspicions surrounding the Russia dealings of the Trump Organization, the Donald J. Trump for President campaign, and various Trump associates and family members continued to cloud the early months of this presidency. As of this writing, the first indictments against close collaborators of the president during the campaign had occurred. But was it all fake news?

The Media, Fake News, and the Importance of Being Earnest

One of the pillars of the Global Liberal Order involves information transparency and freedom of the press. Without them, there can be no truly liberal order either in the political or in the economic sphere. Economic agents— including consumers, labor organizations, investors, and companies—expect to have verifiable information about the state of the economy and the political process. Absent such information, the economy degenerates into crony capitalism and the political system into corruption and clientelism.

Perhaps the biggest challenge to the freedom of the press in recent times is the phenomenon of fake news.

While "print capitalism" had a defining impact on nation building and eventually democracy in Western Europe,[18] there has always been a deep concern about the political role of the media. In the nineteenth century, cheap newsprint technology enabled partisan newspapers to influence politics in ways that were not always conducive to better democratic practices. There were also fears that radio and television might trivialize politics, reducing the substance of political debates in favor of "telegenic" candidates and their simplified slogans, or enabling broadcasting companies to exert a disproportionate amount of political influence. The Internet and digital social media have raised similar concerns. Arguably, digital social media have changed the way in which a certain segment of the electorate finds, consumes, and shares news stories. Most importantly, new technology potentially enables individuals to reach as many readers as the traditional media without the quality controls over the editorial process.[19] Hence the potential for spreading falsehoods, whether intentionally or not.

According to recent research, fake news played a relevant part in the 2016 U.S. presidential election. About "62 percent of U.S. adults get news on social media [. . .], the most popular fake news stories were more widely shared on Facebook than the most popular mainstream news stories [. . .], many people who see fake news stories report that they believe them [. . .], and the most discussed fake news stories tended to favor Donald Trump over Hillary Clinton."[20] In spite of the consternation caused by fake news, the impact on the election may have been relatively small because very few American adults (14 percent) consider social media to be their most important source of election news and the average adult saw and remembered just 1.14 fake stories. Given that research shows each additional TV campaign ad changes vote tallies by about 0.02 percent, the impact of fake news is also in the hundredths of a percentage point, much smaller than Trump's margin of victory.[21] Still, Facebook and Google decided to remove from their platforms sites that publish fake news.

More troubling than fake news is the growing mistrust that the public has developed of the traditional media, and the sustained attacks that they sustained from candidate and President Trump. A survey conducted by the Pew Research Center in mid-2017 showed that the overwhelming majority of Republicans (85 percent) have a negative view of the national news media compared to 58 percent for colleges and universities, 46 percent for labor unions, and 37 percent for banks and financial institutions. It is shocking to learn that Democrats are split, with 46 percent having a negative view of the media and 44 percent a positive one. In fact, more Democrats have a positive view of labor unions and colleges than of the media.[22]

The decline in the public's trust of the traditional media has much to do with the overall polarization of American politics since the 1980s, which has made media outlets more partisan as well. Numerous media companies have launched programming and entire channels catering to partisan audiences, with conservative radio talk shows and Fox News as prominent examples on one side of the spectrum and MSNBC on the other. For instance, the Pew Research Center found that 40 percent of Trump voters say their main source of news is Fox News, while Clinton voters had no such marked preference for any specific outlet, with CNN being the most preferred at 18 percent.

Facebook was the main source for 7 percent of Trump voters and 8 percent of Clinton voters.[23]

The dogmatism and intransigence of technocratic elites, the opportunistic behavior of nationalist-populist politicians, and the polarization of the media have distorted and impoverished the analysis of the virtues and the limitations of Version 2.0 of the Global Liberal Order. As we shall see in the next chapter, the debate has turned negative and prone to mystifications of all sorts.

Intimidating and Suppressing Voters: A Global Tour

The crisis of liberal democracy at the turn of the twenty-first century was exacerbated not just by the rise of nationalist-populist politicians but also by the extensive use of political tactics as old as elections themselves. Efforts to win at the polls through voter intimidation and suppression became so widespread as to threaten the quality of democratic life, turning some democratic systems into semiauthoritarian "anocracies," regimes that are theoretically democratic but not so in practice. Intimidation consists of creating a climate in which voters, individually or as a group, fear negative consequences from going to the polls or from voting for certain candidates. Suppression involves preventing people from voting.

The problem of voter intimidation is pervasive in Africa. According to the Afro-Barometer survey, nearly half of all eligible voters feared violence during elections, and 16 percent reported being offered money or valuable goods in exchange for their vote. In Latin America the proportion of people who received such offers was similar.[24] In the United States, there were increasingly frequent reports of voter intimidation through partisan poll watchers, polling site equipment malfunction or chaos, and aggressive questioning of a person's qualifications to vote. These problems reportedly affected areas with larger minority populations or where the outcome was anticipated to be close, such as in Florida or Pennsylvania.

Some of these developments were made possible by the Supreme Court decision in 2013 to strike down several sections of the Voting Rights Act, which led to nine Southern states approving voter ID laws, and closing or relocating eight hundred polling sites.[25] Voter suppression has also been achieved indirectly through district gerrymandering, the practice of redrawing electoral district boundaries to dilute the voting power of the opposing party across many districts or to pack the voting power of one's own party in one district, or both. Other tactics involve hijacking or merging two districts where the incumbents belong to the opposing party, and kidnapping or moving areas with strong support for the opposing-party incumbent to another district.

Gerrymandering has been practiced in most democracies around the world for decades. Most European countries, Canada and Australia have in recent years reduced the phenomenon by appointing bipartisan or independent commissions to redraw electoral districts. In the United States, by contrast, the practice continues to be widespread, and it is the only major democracy to allow politicians to redefine such boundaries, with the only constraint that gerrymandering cannot target a specific ethnic or minority group. The fact that some states gain population while others lose it at each decennial census creates an opportunity to redistrict given that the Constitution requires districts to be balanced. As a result, some states lose districts and others win them. In addition, population moves within states, creating further needs to redistrict. In most states, a committee made of legislators from the majority party proposes a new electoral map and brings it to the legislature for a vote. Gerrymandering is nowadays practiced by both Republicans and Democrats. New technologies like mapping software and fine-grained block-by-block data analysis have transformed gerrymandering into a science, although some of the machine-generated redistricting is so aggressive that it often fails to survive in the maze of ensuing legal challenges.[26]

Strict photo ID laws in some U.S. states have been commonly linked with attempts to suppress voting by the poor, who often lack such documents. Since 2005, fifteen states adopted such laws, mostly in the South and the Rust Belt corridor from Pennsylvania to Indiana and Wisconsin, plus North Dakota. Most of these instances refer to states with recent Republican control of the legislative and the executive branches. While photo ID laws tend to reduce turnout, it is not clear that the effect is large enough to swing electoral outcomes. The states that adopted such laws have had historically low turnout, and the opposing party (i.e., the Democrats) tend to allocate resources to minimize the impact. Moreover, many Democratic-leaning voters respond to the laws by mobilizing and voting. These countervailing effects may wear out over time, meaning that the full effect of voter suppression may not have yet occurred. More delicate is the issue of racial and ethnic discrimination. While only 7 percent of whites and 10 percent of Latinos report not having a driver's license, the proportion among African Americans is 21 percent. The discriminatory effect increases if one considers the requirements for the license to be valid at the polls, namely, not being expired, matching the registration address, and matching the registration name. Among whites, 16 percent do not hold a license that would enable them to vote, compared to 27 percent for Latinos and 37 percent for African Americans. Thus, more than one-third of all blacks would not be able to vote if strict photo ID laws were approved across the country. Most strikingly, whites are less likely (by seven percentage points) to be asked for an ID at the polls even if one is required.[27]

Meddling in Elections

The last actor that has emerged as a disrupter of the Global Liberal Order is Russia in its efforts to influence elections not just in its own sphere of influence among the former Soviet republics and Soviet-bloc countries but also in the United States and Western Europe. According to a declassified version of a major report by the Office of the Director of National Intelligence, "Russian efforts to influence the 2016 U.S. presidential election represent the most recent expression of Moscow's longstanding desire to undermine the U.S.-led liberal democratic order, but these activities demonstrated a significant escalation in directness, level of activity, and scope of effort compared to previous operations." The assessment indicated that President Putin personally ordered an influence campaign, and that "the Russian Government developed a clear preference for President-elect Trump. The tools included covert cyber activity targeting the Democratic Party and state and local electoral boards, state-funded media, third-party intermediaries, and paid social media users.[28]

In Western Europe, several countries have been forced to take extraordinary measures to prevent Russian hacking of government offices and election servers, including Denmark, the Netherlands, and the United Kingdom. In France, Russian operatives tried to undermine the image of the leading candidate, Macron, and hack his campaign's servers.[29] In Eastern Europe, Russian efforts to undermine democracy and advance its own interests escalated as tensions and crises proliferated in Georgia, the Baltics, and Ukraine, among others.[30]

Russia benefits from the free trade that the Global Liberal Order guarantees. But Putin's own survival as a politician is based on cultivating the perception that Russia is surrounded by hostile countries. Putin also benefits from creating an image of himself as an influential leader in the world. Allegations of electoral interference seem to solidify his image among hard-core supporters.

While Russia, or the Soviet Union, has meddled with elections around the world, it is no less true that the United States and its European allies have done as much, from the 1948 Italian parliamentary election to the 2009 Afghan presidential election and the 2016 Egyptian presidential election. According to a recent study, between 1946 and 2000 the United States interfered in more than twice as many foreign elections as the Soviet Union or Russia did, excluding instances in which the strategy of influence was to promote a coup d'état. Out of a total of 937 electoral contests around the world during that time period, the United States interfered with 81 of them, and the Soviet Union/Russia with 36. Tellingly, Russian interference declined sharply during the 1990s, while U.S. meddling increased. In Asia, 21 percent of the elections were the target of interferences, followed by Europe with 16 percent. Contrary to the conventional wisdom, only 13 percent of elections in Latin America, 10 percent in the Middle East, and 3 percent in Africa were affected.[31] American favoritism and meddling continued into the twenty-first century, especially in countries such as Kenya, Libya, Macedonia, and Egypt. The evidence indicates that such interferences do help favored candidates, and that overt interventions are more effective than covert ones.[32]

While cold-warriors argued that defending democracy sometimes required taking such extraordinary measures as election meddling and promoting coups d'état, it is clear that from the perspective of the twenty-first century, foreign interference with elections undermines the Global Liberal Order. The United States and Europe should not use a double standard whereby Russia's actions are reprehensible while their own are not.

Playing Defense on Human Rights and Civil Rights

As if voter intimidation and suppression, and election meddling were not enough, the causes of human rights and civil rights also came under attack. In Europe and the United States segments of the population and community groups that care about individual rights had to mobilize in order to slow down the onslaught and to send a clear message. The women's march on Washington and other U.S. cities in January 2017 was a powerful example of this countermovement.

Around the world, threats to human rights escalated with the growth in the number of failed states and of anocracies. In parts of Africa and the Middle East violations of human rights have become routine, especially in the midst of civil conflicts or wars. Children's right to education is simply ignored, with increasing numbers of them being forced into becoming soldiers and/or sex slaves. Women have not fared any better, with laws grounded in religious beliefs undermining their status and independence in an alarmingly large number of countries.

In Europe and, especially, the United States, the nationalist-populist reaction against liberalism has extended into civil rights such as voting rights, women's rights, and LGBT rights. The most blatant aggressions have taken place in countries such as Russia or Turkey, where strongmen have found it politically and electorally expedient to curtail civil rights. In Eastern Europe some countries have moved, albeit slowly, toward imposing limits, while in Western Europe there have been few if any negative developments.

The most worrisome case is the United States, where the election of Donald Trump has resulted in a series of attempts, some of them successful, at limiting civil rights in general, and those of women, minorities, and the LGBT community in particular, threatening the hard-won legislation that sought to guarantee equality in society.

Liberalism lies at the root of one strand of feminist theory and practice. Unlike radical feminism, it stops well short of arguing that the structure of society needs to be completely overhauled in order for women's rights to be effectively protected against patriarchy. Instead, liberal feminism focuses on leveling the playing field by eliminating obstacles to women's advancement, especially in the labor market and inside corporations and the government. Admittedly, progress toward that goal has been slow, but nonetheless significant.

Liberalism has also underpinned the fight for LGBT rights, although it is fair to recognize that mere tolerance does not provide for a robust defense of LGBT rights such as, for instance, same-sex marriage and nondiscrimination in schools and the workplace. As Michael Sandel and Carlos Ball have argued, mere neutrality did not provide enough support for the idea of equality for women, minorities, and the LGBT community.[33] Other tools of liberal theory and practice were deemed necessary to advance the cause of civil rights, especially those provided by a government inspired by liberal principles.

In the developing world, the socioeconomic status of women was at the center of the debate about economic growth since the 1970s. A Danish economist working for the United Nations, Ester Boserup, published the influential book *Women's Role in Economic Development*, in which she showed the enormous extent to which women contribute to economic development inside and outside of the household.[34] Her work inspired the United Nations Decade for Women (1975–1985) and laid the foundations for the wave of studies and programs arguing that promoting women's role in the economy could become a major contributor to development.[35] Development experts embraced the approach, not only in order to advance gender equality as a goal in its own right, but also to explore ways in which women's economic activities could contribute to economic growth and to economic development. Still, development efforts tended to create a segregated labor market along gender lines, with women clustering in more labor-intensive activities in light manufacturing (e.g., textiles, food-processing) that paid lower wages, or being self-employed in the service sector. By the time of the crisis of 2008, women were still at an economic disadvantage in many parts of the developing world.

The turn of the twenty-first century has proved to be devastating for political moderates, political compromise, and liberalism in general. Some of the fallout was the result of misguided liberal policies, especially those concerning financial matters. Liberal technocrats went too far in promoting free markets as a long-term solution, without paying attention to the short-term negative implications. Simultaneously, technological change erupted with force, disrupting entire industries. Who or what was to be blamed for the mess?

Chapter 4

Allocating the Blame

The new actors onstage—from technocrats to nationalist and populist politicians—were given to making extreme claims about the origins of the problems afflicting citizens in their countries and how to address them. Chief among these was the controversy over free trade. Not far behind was the debate over the key element in Version 2.0 of the Global Liberal Order, namely, free capital flows. Immigration and technology were also presented as culprits.

Is Free Trade Such an Evil?

Free trade is frequently mentioned as a factor in the decline of manufacturing in Europe and the United States. During the 1950s and 1960s, American and European companies and their workers enjoyed the benefits of free trade both in terms of the jobs it created through greater specialization based on exports, and lower prices for consumers. In fact, the Global Liberal Order version 1.0, based on Keynesian policies, was specifically geared toward enhancing the benefits for the working class of the market economy and free merchandise trade. French workers, for instance, could export manufactured goods to Spain while the latter sold them oranges. Charles de Gaulle famously asserted that such trade was mutually beneficial even when Spain was under a dictatorial regime, noting that he had never heard of "a fascist orange." American and European companies, and their workers, made a fortune manufacturing goods for each other's markets and for the developing world.

When the tables were turned, however, and economies in Southern Europe and, especially, East Asia started to churn cheap manufactured goods and sought to sell them in the developed markets of Europe and the United States, the reaction was timid at first, but resolutely hostile later, especially after the oil crises of the 1970s. Protectionism became the norm, especially toward Japan, adopting at times euphemistic forms, including "voluntary export restraints" or enhanced bureaucratic controls at the border.

According to economic theory, trade benefits everyone in the long term. The trouble with free trade is that its negative effects tend to manifest themselves in highly concentrated ways, undermining specific industries and local communities. Thus, Detroit or Birmingham suffered the brunt of it. Meanwhile, other parts of the economy and of the developed world benefited from trade. Free trade always generates winners and losers, especially in the short run. The argument for free trade is about the balance of benefits and costs for the entire economy. Politically, it is always incumbent on the government and the community to look for ways to protect those negatively affected by it, and to provide them with the means to adapt. Free trade can be especially devastating to people above the age of fifty, those with nontransferable skills, and those with limited geographical mobility due to cultural barriers, dual careers, or sunk costs (such as housing). What's unfair about free trade is that it is not uniform in its effects.

Another legitimate argument against free trade is that production in some countries is competitive because of exploitatively low wages, dangerous working conditions, and lax environmental regulations. These ills are commonly referred to as "social dumping." The concept of "fair trade" seeks to address these issues by establishing boundaries to what counts as fair competition in global markets. The use of child labor is also conducive to unfair trade as well as to abuse. International labor conventions, such as those proposed by the International Labor Organization, and ratified by most countries in the world, seek to address these issues. Ratification, however, does not always lead to actual observance and enforcement.

Both the supporters of the Global Liberal Order and opponents of free trade join in condemning unfair trade, although the former offer a narrower definition of what counts as unfair than the latter. At a time when liberalism is in retreat, adopting a broad definition would not only benefit workers but also rebuild popular support for free trade. Unfortunately, governments often fail to incorporate enough safeguards in trade agreements to protect workers. Evidence of this problem are the frequent consumer boycotts of brands that involve manufacturing in countries where child labor or poor working conditions occur.

Chapter 4

What Counts as an American-Made Product?

A key concept in the nationalist-populist critique of the
Global Liberal Order is that of the "homemade product."
Without a clear definition, the critique becomes less inci-
sive. The problem for protectionist arguments is that there
appears no such thing as a 100-percent homemade product. There is always a certain proportion of a product's
final value that comes from abroad because some input,
part, component, or treatment has a foreign origin.

The debate over trade protectionism in the United
States has frequently run into this basic definitional problem. According to a recent study by the U.S. Department
of Commerce, the manufacturing industries in the United
States that use the least foreign inputs to generate their
output are computers and electronics (12 percent foreign
inputs), apparel (13), wood (13), food and beverages (14),
and chemicals (14). By contrast, some industries need
larger proportions of imported inputs, including automobiles (29) and primary metals (25).[1]

The case of automobiles is especially important
because of its impact on the economy and the frequency
with which it gets discussed in the media and turned into
an issue by politicians. According to the Made in America Auto Index calculated by the Kogod School of Business at American University, the models with the highest
total domestic (i.e., American) content are the Chevrolet
Traverse, the Buick Enclave, and the GMC Acadia, with
85.5 percent. Some foreign-branded cars have proportions as high as 78.5 percent, including the Honda CR-V,
Ridgeline, and Pilot, and the Acura RDX, the Kia Optima,
and the Toyota Camry.[2] This means that even the most

"American" automobiles have significant proportions of their value added through imported parts and components, something that would be expected from the international division of labor.

One might argue that the U.S. economy is better off if more consumers purchase goods with a greater proportion of Made in America value, but it is clear that at least some American workers benefit from the purchases of goods with a lower proportion. Thus, it is always the case that if a consumer switches from one product to another, there will be some American firms and workers that benefit while others do not. If Toyota sells more cars in the U.S. market, that will benefit workers in Tennessee, where some of their models are assembled. If BMW's sales increase, employment in South Carolina may increase. Or if Ford's sales go up, Michigan workers might benefit. Given how complex the U.S. and global economies have become, there are always winners and losers.

Has NAFTA Undermined American Economic Well-Being?

This analysis becomes even more complicated when considering the effects of trade blocs. Most of the debate in the United States about the North American Free Trade Agreement has focused on job losses, given the large decline in manufacturing jobs that took place in the 1990s. But has NAFTA actually contributed significantly to that outcome? It seems accurate to maintain that around eight hundred thousand jobs may have moved south of the border to Mexico, a country with lower base wages and less stringent business and environmental regulations.[3] The conventional wisdom is that these job losses make NAFTA an agreement contrary to the national interests of the United States and to those of the American working class.

As usual, the realities surrounding NAFTA are far more complex than the simple equation "NAFTA = Job Migration to Mexico" seems to suggest. This trade bloc has also created jobs in the United States: anywhere between two and four million jobs depend on trade with Mexico. Indeed, what most politicians, analysts, and commentators forget is that the NAFTA has created tens of thousands of high-paying jobs in the United States at the expense of workers in countries like Germany, Japan, and South Korea. Companies from these countries used to ship their goods to the U.S. market but now make them here. A little-known fact about NAFTA is that, while the agreement provides for free trade among its three signatories, it is a protectionist trade pact relative to the rest of the world.

Take the example of automobiles. Before NAFTA came into effect at the beginning of 1994, exports of automobiles from the above-mentioned countries were literally flooding the U.S. market.[4] But NAFTA made it more expensive for European and East Asian automobile companies to export because the North American local content requirement was raised from 50 percent to 62.5 percent. This meant that in order to avoid tariffs, a vehicle sold in the United States (or Canada or Mexico for that matter) had to incorporate more value in its components originating from within the NAFTA zone. At the same time, the rules under NAFTA as to how that local content requirement is calculated became more stringent.

Automobile companies responded to NAFTA's protectionist stance swiftly. Within months, the Japanese, South

Korean, and German makers were drawing plans to shift production away from their respective home countries and set up assembly facilities in the United States. Toyota established new manufacturing capacity in Indiana (starting production in 1990), BMW in South Carolina (1994), Mercedes-Benz in Alabama (1997), Honda in Alabama (2001), Hyundai in Alabama (2005), KIA in Georgia (2008), and Volkswagen in Tennessee (2011). Each of these assembly plants required the co-location of hundreds of suppliers. If there are about eight hundred thousand U.S. workers engaged in automobile assembly and component manufacturing, a bit more than a third work for foreign-owned companies.[5] Many of those jobs would, without NAFTA, be located in Europe or East Asia.

The political aspects of NAFTA's protectionism should not be overlooked. President Trump campaigned on a platform that leaned heavily on the narrative of Midwestern unemployment. This is only part of the story, however. Investments by European and East Asian firms have benefited workers and their communities in the United States—but not necessarily in the Rust Belt. Instead, they preferred regions with weaker unions and more favorable tax treatment, available in states like Alabama, Georgia, South Carolina, or Tennessee. In addition, the original intention behind the protectionist treatment of foreign-made automobiles was to help the Big Three—General Motors, Ford, and Chrysler. Yet NAFTA has largely failed to benefit American auto companies, which increasingly found it difficult to compete. In some cases it actually had the opposite effect, shifting production offshore (including to Mexico), and focusing on trucks, minivans, and SUVs, for which they had, at least temporarily, a competitive advantage.

In more ways than one, agreements such as NAFTA brought about a reconfiguration of the international division of labor, shifting jobs from the United States to Mexico, and from Europe and Asia toward the United States. In addition, it created millions of jobs on both sides of the U.S.-Mexico border. What appears to be clear is that the traditional unionized labor strongholds of the Midwest lost to the Southern and Southwestern states, with the labor movement losing strength. Eventually, these changes led to a tectonic shift in political alignments and electoral outcomes.

Unlike some of the talk coming out of the Trump administration and some segments of the Democratic Party, however, the solution to job losses is not to fall back on protectionism. In fact, such policies will ultimately hurt consumers, make companies lazy, reduce the incentives for innovation, and encourage interest groups who benefit from the protections to lobby so that they remain in place. The solution must instead be to take care of those who are negatively affected and help them adapt to the changing economy. Neither a revived Global Liberal Order nor its polar opposite will bring manufacturing jobs back. In the United States, there has been a generalized failure to take care of workers displaced by technological change. Spending on so-called active labor market policies—worker retraining, job-search assistance, employment incentives, direct employment, etc.—has declined in the United States from 0.26 percent of GDP in 1985 to 0.12 percent by 2015. Among OECD countries, only Mexico and Chile spend less. At the high end of the spectrum, Sweden and Denmark spend more than ten times as much.[6]

The Real Culprit: Short-Term Capital Flows

In addition to free trade and trade blocs, short-term capital flows are oftentimes blamed for the ills of globalization in general and the Global Liberal Order Version 2.0 in particular. Both Adam Smith and Karl Marx, from their own peculiar standpoints, understood the intricacies of capital movements in the global economy. In *The Wealth of Nations*, Smith noted that "the proprietor of stock is properly a citizen of the world, and is not necessarily attached to any particular country."[7] A century later, Marx pointed out that capitalists benefit not only from their ability to shift investments from one location to another but also from investing in underdeveloped areas: "The rate of profit is higher [in the colonies] due to backward development, and likewise the exploitation of labor."[8] Both recognized that capitalism unfolded on a global scale, and that capital moving across borders was a key factor, with rather distinctive consequences.

The theory that, in order for the market economy to deliver its goods, capital needs to roam freely across the global economic landscape has been attacked by a long list of politicians, economists, and social critics. Perhaps one of the most articulate critiques is by Jagdish Bagwhati, a renowned trade economist, who argued that

> when we penetrate the fog of implausible assertions that surrounds the case for free capital mobility, we realize that the idea and the ideology of free trade and its benefits [. . .] have, in effect, been hijacked by the proponents of capital mobility. They have been used

to bamboozle us into celebrating the new world of trillions of dollars moving about daily in a borderless world, creating gigantic economic gains, rewarding virtue and punishing profligacy. The pretty face presented to us is, in fact, a mask that hides the warts and wrinkles underneath.[9]

In his blistering criticism of free capital flows, and implicit defense of free trade, Bagwhati is not alone. Carmen Reinhardt and Kenneth Rogoff, two leading economists and authors of a best-selling book on financial crises, also argued that cross-border capital flows make it more likely for domestic banks to go bust when portfolio investors suddenly desert the country in anticipation of a currency realignment, changes in monetary policies, or simply poor economic conditions. Using data on sixty-six countries since 1800, they show that banking crises were rare during periods of low cross-border capital mobility (1800–1880 and 1945–1980), while they were quite frequent during periods of high capital mobility (1880–1940 and 1980 to the present time). During the latter periods, up to one-third of all countries experienced systemic banking crises with a significant number of defaults.[10]

Even more tellingly, one IMF study concluded in 2016 that among countries that experienced a surge in short-term capital inflows, 20 percent suffered from either a banking or a currency crisis compared to 7 percent among countries that experienced no such surge. The difference is even more pronounced if one considers the simultaneous occurrence of a banking and a currency crisis, with the proportion jumping from 1.5 to 7 percent. Moreover, income inequality on average more than doubles two years after the crisis, and nearly quadruples five years later.[11] In general, liberalization of capital flows has been found to approximately double income inequality for up to five years after it occurs.[12]

These pernicious effects of short-term capital flows have done much damage to the legitimacy of the Global Liberal Order, especially because they have grown so quickly. Foreign portfolio assets grew from 25 percent of global GDP in 1997 to 70 percent in 2007, declined with the crisis to a low of 50 percent in 2008, and then recovered to 62 percent by the end of 2013, a level more than twice as high than in 1997.[13]

It is important to note that free trade and free capital flows have had very different effects on inequality: "Trade globalization has exerted an equalizing impact, whereas financial globalization has been associated with widening income disparities."[14] This empirical fact has been utterly absent from the political debates of the last few years. It indicates that if there is a culprit involving cross-border transactions, all fingers should point to capital flows, not free trade.

Another problematic angle in the debate about free capital flows has been the idea that it makes sense to subject governments to the discipline of the market so as to curb their profligacy. Conditions in the government bond markets certainly became a constraint on economic policy making, leading to accusations that unelected money managers have more influence over government programs than elected officials. The liberal framework does not provide for a solution to this issue given that its economic version would be consistent with market-based controls on government behavior, but its political advocates would insist upon governmental autonomy to make decisions that improve the lot of the citizenry. As usual, the problem is eminently political in nature, and some kind of a balance between the two opposing considerations needs to be struck.

The "Mighty Dollar" and the Enemy Within

The global economy cannot exist without currencies. Since most governments prefer to have one, trade and investment typically take place across currency areas. Also, currency markets exist so that consumers, investors, companies, and governments can engage in international transactions.

Currencies are not made equal. Some of them acquire truly international status, while most others do not. Historically, we observe a pattern of the rise and decline of currencies that are more trusted than others, and hence become cornerstones of the financial and trading world. From the first century BCE to the fourth century CE, the Roman *aureus* was perhaps the currency that came closest to playing the role of an international currency. The Byzantine *solidus* (a great brand name) was widely used in international trade from the fourth to the twelfth centuries. During the Renaissance it was the Florentine *fiorino* that played this essential role, and later came the Dutch *gulden* (seventeenth–eighteenth centuries), followed by the Spanish *real de a ocho*, dubbed the "Spanish dollar" (eighteenth–early nineteenth centuries). In the contemporary period, the world has seen two main international currencies, the British pound sterling and the U.S. dollar.

The importance of the U.S. dollar to the global economy cannot be exaggerated. After all, it is the only currency accepted all over the world, a truly international medium of exchange for private actors and governments alike. It is the unit of account used for valuing many commodities and the dominant currency for trade invoicing. It is also the currency used by many governments to anchor their own local currencies, and the most widely used reserve currency. The dollar has geopolitical and symbolic value as well, enabling the projection of American influence around the world.

And yet, the dollar and the country whose government issues it, and stands by it, is showing clear signs of fatigue. One symptom is the decline in the dollar's share of total allocated reserves, from close to the total in the 1950s to about 64 percent today. The dollar is also becoming less important as an anchor for other currencies. Out of 192 countries, only 20 percent used the dollar as anchor as of 2016, down from 33 percent in 2008. The euro has remained stable at around 13 percent. Meanwhile, other types of arrangements such as targeting a monetary aggregate or inflation, or simply having no nominal anchor, have become more popular.[15] Another sign of the dollar's declining importance is the increasingly introspective, insular posture of the American public and of its federal government, distracted as both of them are by domestic issues and controversies, ranging from taxes and spending to states' rights and the culture wars. The stability provided by the two-party system is also in doubt, and all of that was even before Trump became president.

The most important threat to the global liberal trading system, however, comes from within, and it involves the interplay between trade and capital movements. It is a well-known fact that, in the absence of interplanetary trade, every trade deficit in the world corresponds to a surplus.

If a country enjoys a surplus, there must be at least one other country that has a deficit, and vice versa. The broadest measure of economic exchange between countries is the so-called current account, which includes trade in goods, trade in services, and transfers such as remittances or international aid. By this measure, during the 1980s and 1990s surpluses and deficits in the global economy never exceeded plus or minus 1 percent of the value of the entire global gross product. After 2000, however, the surpluses and deficits skyrocketed to nearly 3 percent, with the U.S. deficit becoming the largest in the world by a wide margin. Imbalances came down considerably after the 2008 crisis, but nowadays they continue to be twice as large as they were in the last two decades of the twentieth century.

Larger deficits in the current account means that there need to be larger capital flows to cover the gap. While investment by companies bridges some of the shortfall, most of the capital flows are portfolio investments, a majority in government-issued bonds. If each year larger capital flows take place to fund the deficits, those countries providing the money accumulate ever larger assets in the form of reserves, while the deficit countries acquire more liabilities. The fact that just a few countries like Germany, China, and Japan enjoy large surpluses not only creates tensions in the world, but it also appears to undermine the basic premise of the Global Liberal Order that everyone benefits from free trade. It seems that a reduction in global trade imbalances would deprive populist and protectionist politicians from some of their best arguments, and it would help supporters of the Global Liberal Order with some room to regroup and come up with new arguments and proposals.

Imbalances basically mean that some countries are doing better than others, and some of them (e.g., China, Germany, Japan, South Korea, etc.) are doing exceptionally well. Large surpluses in China, Germany, and Japan mean that those countries are not spending enough, and are thus preventing the rest of the world from growing at a rate that would be better for them in terms of reducing unemployment or increasing standards of living. In China the high savings rate has been driven by a combination of fear about the lack of old-age protections, and the gender imbalance. The latter—caused by a preference for male children—has encouraged parents to save in order to make their sons more attractive in the marriage market. In Germany, the savings rate is high but has not changed much over the last few decades. What makes the German economy so unique is the moderation shown by labor's economic demands, even when productivity is on the rise. After having trouble digesting technological change and unification with the East during the 1990s, the German economy became a global powerhouse by investing in the labor force, restraining wage growth, and innovating. By the mid-2010s, Germany enjoyed the largest trade surplus in the world, even larger than China's. While it is true that two-thirds of that surplus was generated with the rest of Europe, and Germany had a bilateral deficit in its trade with China, German economic performance was remarkably strong. Moreover, many goods assembled in China for export use German parts and components. For instance, the iPhone is assembled in China, but 36 percent of the value of the components comes from Japan, 18 percent from Germany, and 14 percent from South Korea. These numbers mean that much of the bilateral trade deficit between the United States and China in assembled goods ultimately is a deficit with Japan, Germany, and South Korea.

The resentment about ever-larger trade imbalances is in part what has fueled the protectionist agenda in some European countries and, especially, in the United States, where Trump made it a top policy priority of his administration. As Peking University's Michael Pettis has observed,

> Exporting capital means importing demand, and except in a few restricted and very specific cases, importing capital, especially for rich countries, will mean slower growth and rising unemployment. The "currency wars" that have been much in the news recently are simply "wars" in which countries try desperately to export their unwanted savings to each other.[16]

President Nixon's decision in 1971 to take the dollar off the gold standard made the implications of these imbalances even starker. "Unlike the gold standard or the original Bretton Woods system, these reserve flows have not been fettered by the physical availability of gold; the resulting imbalances are clearly larger and more persistent," mainly because they are driven by the twin decisions of many emerging economies, especially China, "to set the value of their own currencies low enough to engineer large current account surpluses," and to purchase reserve assets from deficit countries.[17] These capital flows do not seem to respond to market incentives because they go to richer countries with lower interest rates and slacking aggregate demand, compared to the emerging markets. *Financial*

Times columnist Martin Wolf has framed the issue in even more dramatic terms, arguing that "the global market for the U.S. dollar is rigged. It is one in which governments are prepared to buy massively, to prevent prices from reaching natural market clearing levels." It is hard to estimate the exact quantitative impact of such distortions. "We do not know how much lower the dollar would have been if there had been no such intervention, but surely it would have been substantially weaker and U.S. monetary policy would have consequently needed to be less expansionary."[18]

Let's Blame It on Outsiders: Immigrants as Scapegoats

As if free trade and short-term capital movements were not enough, international migration has also become the subject of heated debates about globalization and the negative effects on local communities and the working class in the destination countries. The argument about the harm that migration inflicts on local labor markets, however, has serious shortcomings. It is important to note that most of the job losses in developed countries have occurred in the manufacturing sector among workers with intermediate levels of skill. Low-skilled jobs are still plentiful in developed economies, especially in agriculture and the service sector. Demand for highly skilled workers is also strong across the economy. At the same time, most immigrants are either highly skilled or people with few skills. People in developing countries with intermediate levels of skills have plenty of job opportunities available in their communities of origin, and thus decide not to migrate. The labor surplus has to do with people at both extremes of the skill distribution.[19] Thus, and contrary to the conventional wisdom, there is actually very little competition for jobs between immigrants and locals in the developed countries. At the low end in terms of skills, fewer locals than immigrants are willing to take low-paying jobs in agriculture or in the service sector. At the high end of the spectrum, companies in the United States and Europe complain that they cannot find enough qualified workers.

The statistics on how many foreign-born people are employed in the United States by level of education corroborate that immigrants have not stolen jobs away from Americans. About 42 percent of all employees who dropped out of high school are immigrants, and about 29 percent are foreign born among doctoral-degree holders. By contrast, only 15 percent of those with a high school diploma or 10 percent of those with some college education but without a degree are immigrants. Thus, the presence of immigrants in the U.S. labor market preponderates at either end of the skill and education spectrum, but not in the middle. Meanwhile, the number of managerial and technical jobs has increased while the numbers of blue-collar and even clerical jobs have declined sharply.[20]

Data on specific occupations corroborate the general finding that that most immigrants do not compete for jobs with locals. According to the Urban Institute, in the United States the top three occupational groups among immigrants without high school diplomas are maids and housekeepers, cooks, and agricultural laborers. For native workers without a high school diploma the top three are cashiers, drivers of vehicles and trucks, and janitors. While large numbers of both immigrants and natives work as cooks, natives are much more numerous as waiters or waitresses. They both work as janitors, grounds maintenance workers, material movers, and drivers, but there are much greater numbers of immigrants who work as carpenters and many more natives who are employed as health workers.

Most importantly, a high proportion of immigrants become entrepreneurs. While many ventures launched by immigrants are in traditional sectors and rarely employ people outside their immediate or extended family, or circle of friends, foreign-born entrepreneurs play a disproportionate role in the high-tech sector, where thousands if not tens of thousands of jobs might be created. According to the Kauffman Foundation and the Bay Area Council Economic Institute, about 23 percent of all high-tech ventures in the United States are founded by immigrants, a proportion that is as stunningly high as 40 percent in California, 42 percent in Massachusetts, and 45 percent in New Jersey. A comprehensive report from the National Academies found that "immigrants are more innovative than natives; more specifically, high-skilled immigrants raise patenting per capita, which is likely to boost productivity and per capital economic growth," adding that "immigrants appear to innovate more than natives not because of greater inherent ability but due to their concentration in science and engineering fields."[21]

If immigrants competed for the same jobs as natives, then one would observe a decline in the wages for those affected. Myriad studies using different methodologies have been undertaken to illuminate this question. The National Academies concluded that "the impact of immigration on the overall native wage may be small and close to zero." More importantly, most research has found "larger negative effects for disadvantaged groups and for prior immigrants than for natives overall."[22] The latter finding may explain why significant proportions of recent immigrants voted for Trump in the 2016 presidential election in spite of the candidate's demonization of immigration. The native group most exposed to the effects of immigration are high school dropouts, also a key constituency for Trump.

Besides the impact of immigration on the labor market per se, it is also important to note that immigrants tend to be younger on average than the population of the destination countries. To the extent that they work, pay taxes, and make contributions to the social security system, immigrants tend to represent a stabilizing factor in rapidly aging societies. About 72 percent of all international migrants in the world are of working age, compared to 58 percent for the total population.[23] According to one study, immigrants accounted for 47 percent of the increase in the workforce in the United States and 70 percent in Europe since 1990, and they tend to contribute more in taxes than they receive in benefits from government programs.[24]

The National Academies had already concluded in a 1997 report that "the most plausible magnitudes of the impact of immigration on the economy are modest for those [natives] who benefit from immigration, for those who lose from immigration, and for total GDP. The domestic gain [. . .] may be modest relative to the size of the U.S. economy, but it remains a significant positive gain in absolute terms."[25] In its 2017 report, the National Academies observed that, without immigration to the United States, "clearly GDP would be much smaller, and perhaps per capita GDP would be as well—in no small part because the United States would have an older population with a considerably lower percentage of individuals active in the workforce. Other aspects include the fact that "the contributions of immigrants to the labor force reduce the prices of some goods and services, which benefits consumers in a range of sectors including child care, food preparation, hose cleaning and repair, and construction. Moreover, new arrivals and their descendants also provide a major source of demand in sectors such as housing, benefiting residential real estate markets." In sum, "the prospects for long-run economic growth in the United States would be considerably dimmed without the contributions of high-skilled immigrants."[26]

The evidence on the fiscal impact of immigration also contradicts the conventional wisdom that immigrants are a burden on government programs. "At any given age, adult members of the second generation [of immigrants] typically have had a more positive net fiscal impact for all government levels combined than either first or third-plus generation adults." Given the different age distributions, "the third-plus generation has consistently been more expensive to government on a per capita basis than either the first or the second." Most importantly, between 1994 and 2013 the ratio of taxes to benefits "increased for both the first and second generation groups," indicating that over time immigrants are contributing more fiscally than what they are receiving in benefits from government programs. It is worth noting that the fiscal impact of immigrants is more positive at the federal level—given that most of them are of working age—than at the state and local levels, which fund the education of their children.

The National Academies conclude that "an immigrant and a native-born person with similar characteristics [e.g., age, education, income] will likely have about the same fiscal impact."[27]

In spite of its net economic benefits, immigration frequently leads to social and political problems to the extent that identities clash, residential segregation grows, and social marginalization becomes the norm. Nowhere are these problems more visible than in France, a country that prides itself on having impeccable liberal political values. The assimilation of immigrants has also spurred heated debates in the United States, where the very national narrative has oftentimes been written around the image of the oppressed and destitute immigrant who yearns for freedom and opportunity. Liberal thinking about immigration has struggled to adapt to changing conceptions of assimilation.[28] Starting with the classic (and fairly romantic) view of the "melting pot," where immigrant groups slowly but surely converge on the majority group in terms of values, norms, behaviors, and even characteristics by virtue of progressive identification with the host society and intermarriage, liberal thought about immigration has come a long way. The limitations and tensions of this perspective, which was en vogue during the 1920s, became readily apparent during the 1960s as research documented the existence of long-lasting discrimination and barriers to employment in the mainstream of the economy by immigrant groups.

By the 1960s, policy makers realized that assimilation often took longer than two generations, and often led to the formation of disadvantaged racial or ethnic minorities. With the passage of time, liberal thinking about immigration turned more optimistic, embracing a so-called segmented assimilation theory during the 1990s, a perspective that recognized the existence of multiple pathways to assimilation depending on ethnicity, religious background, socioeconomic status, family resources, and social capital. It was not until the turn of the twenty-first century that scholars, policy makers, and the public at large realized that assimilation was being delayed, and even derailed, by lingering identities, reliance on racial or ethnic networks to secure employment and advance economically, and in many cases and situations outright hostility and discrimination by the majority. It was against this backdrop that migration became the central theme in political debates and elections in the United States and Europe.

Unfortunately, only a small part of the debate has focused on what might be the best model of immigration policy. Most political discourse has dangerously evolved into xenophobia. Countries around the world differ much in terms of the policies they have pursued, with varying results. From the point of view of the Global Liberal Order, the central issue when it comes to designing an effective, humane, and just immigration policy has to do with whether the political or the economic aspects of liberalism should take precedence. The most extreme manifestation of a politically defined liberal immigration policy would have quotas as its central element. Given that political liberalism depends on a strict definition of national boundaries and citizenship, quotas offer a solution that appears to be objective, balanced, and sensitive to the need for both controlling immigration and offering freedom and opportunity to at least some of those who lack it. Another model congruent with political liberalism prioritizes immigration in terms of family reunion, ethnic or linguistic similarity, and historical or colonial ties.

From the standpoint of economic liberalism, however, the purest model of immigration policy would be demand driven, and should serve the needs of employers in the destination country. This model was historically pioneered by the United States and Germany. A less radical approach involves "planned immigration," typically based on a point system that prioritizes immigrants in terms of their skills, education, work experience, and age. This model was pioneered by Australia and Canada, with the United Kingdom and France having adopted some of its features. In practice, most countries in the world combine elements from the quota-based, demand-driven, and planned models.

The Machines Are Taking Over

If immigration is not the main reason for job losses among workers with intermediate levels of skill, one must turn to either trade or technology as the most important threats. Trade is certainly behind some of the job losses, but myriad empirical studies confirm that technological change is a far more important factor. According to one study, up to 88 percent of all job losses in manufacturing since 2000 were due to productivity growth, mainly driven by technological change.[29] Most importantly, the idea that manufacturing in the United States is on the decline is inaccurate. The largest rate of increase in manufacturing output since the 1920s occurred during the mid to late 1990s, coinciding with the coming into effect of NAFTA and other bilateral free trade agreements, a fact that is generally ignored. After a brief recession in 2001, output continued to climb until the 2008 crisis. By 2014, the U.S. manufacturing economy had fully recovered. The most important change, however, had to do with productivity. Compared to 1980, by 2015 about 40 percent *fewer* workers were employed in U.S. manufacturing. Over the same period, real output (adjusted for inflation) grew by more than 250 percent.[30]

If technology is mostly to blame, then we should observe that occupations performing routine tasks are the most affected, given that they are easier to automate. That is exactly what the statistics show. The number of people employed in routine manual jobs in the United States stood at 28 million in 1983. By 2015 that number had slightly increased to 30 million. Similarly, the number of routine cognitive (i.e., nonmanual) grew from 28 to 33 million. By contrast, nonroutine manual jobs increased from 14 to 27 million, and nonroutine cognitive from 28 to a whopping 57 million.[31] While there has been no net job destruction within the routine occupational groups, the economy is much greater today, manufacturing output included, and yet those occupations have remained flat.

The implications for the 2016 presidential election were quite direct. Using data at the county level, the political analysis website FiveThirtyEight found that unemployment could not explain Trump's advantage over Clinton. However, the share of a county's jobs that are routine clearly differentiated between counties that supported Trump from those that supported Clinton. Thus, in counties in which less than 40 percent of jobs are routine, Clinton enjoyed up to a 30 percentage point advantage in votes, while in those with 50 percent of jobs being routine

Trump had more than a 35 point advantage.[32] It seems safe to conclude that, to a very large extent, the presidential election was driven by the effects of technology, present and future, on the labor market.

One example might help underscore the widespread economic and political implications of technological change. In 29 of the 50 states of the union, truck drivers constitute the largest occupational group, with either software developers, primary school teachers, farmers, secretaries, nursing aides, retail clerks, customer service representatives, or lawyers taking the top spot in the remaining states.[33] According to a government study, between 1.5 and 2.2 million light and heavy truck drivers are at risk of losing their jobs as a result of autonomous vehicle technology, or between 60 and 90 percent of the total employed in 2015. If one adds bus drivers, taxi drivers, chauffeurs, and self-employed drivers, the potential total of jobs lost to technology could top 3 million.[34] Focusing on the nearly 1.7 million heavy truck drivers in the United States, who live mostly in small towns in states outside the Northeast, the consequences are mind boggling. Entire communities might be affected, given that at least as many induced support and service jobs are also at stake. These blue-collar small towns and rural areas could witness a sea change in their local politics as the jobs disappear, with massive implications for state-level and even electoral-college political dynamics.

Technological change tends to interact with other trends such as demography or migration. Consider the example of Japan, a country with a low fertility rate, rising life expectancy, and very low levels of immigration. As the number of people above age seventy soars, so is the demand for gadgets and devices that enable that age group to continue enjoying life. The latest trend is for home robotics. While Japanese culture favors innovation and there is a shortage of capable companies that design and make robots, the single most important driver is that it is hard for the elderly in Japan to secure the kind of care they need. In Europe and the United States most of the labor hired for such a task are immigrants. In its absence, automation becomes a solution. The same process is taking place at the low end of the age distribution. While in the United States and Europe immigrants are the most likely babysitters, in Japan robotics offers an attractive alternative to the very high costs of hiring workers for that purpose.

Autonomous vehicle technology and robotics are just two fields that are rapidly evolving. The sharing economy is likely to revolutionize labor and service markets as more people become willing to share assets such as automobiles, homes, parking spaces, storage areas, home appliances, outdoor gear, and even clothes and accessories. According to data collected by Nielsen and reported by Statista, Europe and the United States lag behind the rest of the world by 30 percentage points in terms of the proportion of people who are willing to share their own assets or to share from others.[35] This means that the impact of sharing on automobile production, hotel employment, and other parts of the economy might be much greater in the future, especially as the population grows older, given that empty-nesters are more prone to sharing assets. In addition, people who rely on a state pension may find it challenging to make ends meet, and thus may turn to offering their assets to the sharing economy. Across all age groups, stagnating incomes in Europe and the United States have induced people to participate in the sharing economy. For instance, slightly more than half of all Uber drivers work less than fifteen hours per week.

3D printing is still in its infancy, but analysts anticipate breakthroughs in the near future, including the possibility of printing metal parts.[36] This technology could transform the ways in which companies interact with their suppliers, reducing the need for inventories and allowing for a more efficient use of materials. Most crucially, it would reduce demand for transportation and endanger some of the most skilled and best-paying blue-collar occupations. The political implications could be as large as the economic ones. At the same time, 3D printing might help isolated communities in rural areas, and might reduce the carbon footprint by streamlining transportation.

Harder to predict are the consequences of the rapidly evolving universe of nanotechnologies, which involve the manipulation of matter on an atomic, molecular, or supra-molecular scale. Some of these technologies will help the world economize on natural resources and become more sustainable, including more durable materials, higher-strength composites, and energy-efficient building materials. Others have major implications for labor markets, including nanorobotics in general, and nanomedical applications in particular. Programmable matter, such as fabrics that adapt to temperature in the environment, will also open new horizons. Inevitably, some occupations will be severely affected, while new types of jobs are created.

Equally unpredictable in terms of its effects on the labor market are the technologies involved in the Internet of Things, which consists of a large number of interconnected sensors and other devices to improve the functioning of manufacturing, mining, energy systems, transportation, retail, vehicles, homes, offices, and even people. The ecosystem required to implement a true Internet of Things is expansive, including not just the devices but data transmission and storage facilities, analysis hubs, and feedback loops. Arguably, a large number of jobs will be created to support this mammoth infrastructure. While it is not clear that jobs will be destroyed, it is likely that many workers will need to adapt to the implementation of this new technology. For instance, the property and casualty segment within the insurance industry could be drastically transformed, enabling companies to collect data in real time, and calculating premiums based not on historical data and demographics but on actual behavior. Thus, an automobile insurance customer may prefer to agree to be monitored if he or she believes that the premiums calculated through proxies such as age and gender are too high.

The development of artificial intelligence (AI), even if it does not reach some of the most exhilarating prospects and hype, will also be transformational. In 1997 Gary Kasparov was defeated by IBM's Deep Blue. A year later, Tiger Electronics developed a robotic toy with voice-recognition technology. In 2000 Honda launched ASIMO, a humanoid robot serving as a multifunctional personal assistant. In 2011 Apple incorporated Siri into its smartphones. AI facilitates the management of complex systems, such as expert systems, partially eliminating the need for human thinking. The Internet of Things will also develop quickly. It is precisely in this area that learning machines become relevant, especially in areas like health, diagnosis and treatment, agriculture, energy management, transportation, housework, safety, and security.

Perhaps the most far-reaching effect on the labor market will come from the recording technologies known as the "blockchain." The market economy involves billions of daily transactions to which there are at least two parties such as a buyer and a seller, an insurer and an insured, or a borrower and a lender. Verifying that a document, record, title to ownership, or contract existed at some time will also be easier and cheaper with this technology. Budget management will also be simplified if there is a registry that shows how much money is available to spend and how much has already been spent on what. Until now, the registries or ledgers containing all of those records were centralized and controlled by an entity or person trusted by all users or, most frequently, created by the state, such as an office of property records. These technologies "present opportunities in all kinds of public services such as health and welfare payments and, at the frontier of blockchain development, are self-executing contracts paving the way for companies that run themselves without human intervention." The most tantalizing potential of blockchains is that they "shift some control over daily interactions with technology away from central elites, redistributing it among users. In so doing, they make systems more transparent and, perhaps, more democratic."[37]

In its initial stages, blockchain technologies have been used to create digital currencies, of which Bitcoin is just one example among many. While potentially revolutionary in their own right, the true earth-shattering development would combine digital currencies with the smart contracts, digital record management, and decentralized autonomous organizations, all supported by the blockchain. Smart contracts with clauses or payments triggered automatically depending on deadlines or events is another possibility. Tax collection might also be made less complex. In general, the management of supply chains would be simplified and accelerated though a combination of the mechanisms involving contract execution, record keeping, tracking, payment collection, and restocking.

Blockchain technologies may also help address a decades-old problem involving property rights. The liberal market economy depends on well-defined and well-protected property rights. All manner of economic transactions involve establishing and transferring property rights over assets, merchandise, and other valuables. Innovation and research depend crucially on the incentives to invest time, money, and effort on pursuing new possibilities in the hope of obtaining a profit. Piracy of intellectual property, from music to pharmaceutical drugs, has beset entire industries. Blockchains could protect both consumers and rights holders from piracy and copycats.

Another application would relate to the interaction between government agencies and citizens, between corporations and shareholders, or between political parties and their members. Engagement and turnout might increase, although digital accessibility is a concern that could increase inequality. In fact, with blockchain technology voter participation might be even higher among the better educated and more sophisticated groups of individuals who already have higher participation rates.

The impact of blockchains on the labor market will be profound. Historically, liberal capitalism, based as it is in contract law and record keeping, has given rise to many different kinds of occupations that act as intermediaries handling diverse aspects of economic and financial transactions, especially in terms of the trading, clearing, verification, fulfillment, settlement, and record keeping involved. These occupations employ tens of millions of people worldwide. A decentralized, public, distributed ledger that sits online, accessible to all, would rule many of the intermediaries out of existence, simply circumventing them. The service sector, including some well-paid jobs, would be transformed forever.

Each of these technological breakthroughs and disruptions could have implications for the Global Liberal Order, which considers the dynamism of the innovation-based market economy as the engine of human advancement and well-being. The initial formulation of economic liberalism by Adam Smith in 1776 focused on the "invisible hand" of the market. This classic view neglected the dynamic and at the same time disruptive role that technology and entrepreneurship play in the modern market economy. Writing in 1942, Joseph Schumpeter coined the term "creative destruction" in reference to this fundamental process of technological change, alerting the world to the inherently corrosive nature of capitalism and the market economy:

> Capitalism [. . .] is by nature a form or method of economic change and not only never is but never can be stationary. The fundamental impulse that sets and keeps the capitalist engine in motion comes from the new consumers' goods, the new methods of production or transportation, the new markets, the new forms of industrial organization that capitalist enterprise creates. [. . .] The opening up of new markets, foreign or domestic, and the organizational development from

the craft shop and factory to such concerns as U.S. Steel illustrate the same process of industrial mutation [. . .] that incessantly revolutionizes the economic structure from within, incessantly destroying the old one, incessantly creating a new one. This process of Creative Destruction is the essential fact about capitalism.[38]

Unfortunately, that creative destruction brings inequality and other problems along with its purported benefits. A recent IMF study concluded that "technological progress alone explains most of the 0.45 percent average annual increase in the Gini coefficient [a measure of income inequality] from the early 1980s" to the mid-2000s. "Trade and financial globalization and financial deepening contributed a further 0.1 percent a year each [. . .], offset by almost equivalent reductions in the Gini coefficient from increased access to education and a shift of employment away from agriculture." New technology tends to favor skilled workers, thus exacerbating the so-called skills gap. According to the IMF, the increase in income inequality due to the diffusion of information and telecommunications technologies has affected both developed and developing countries, although the effect has been far smaller in Latin America than in Asia.[39]

The steam engine, artificial fibers, antibiotics, nuclear fission, or the transistor changed the economy, including labor markets, and they also transformed culture, politics, and geopolitics. The contemporary equivalents include a bewildering array of technologies that promise to bring both widespread benefits and rampant disruption. The Global Liberal Order may not survive unless a Version 3.0 that is congruent with the new technological, economic, and political realities can be devised. This is the case because innovation and disruption are the heart of the liberal market economy. Yet, unleashing those forces without restraint tends to create inequality and social and political frictions, and to generate winners and losers.

Chapter 5

What Needs to Be Done?

The Global Liberal Order was supposed to bring economic well-being and political freedoms to everyone. During the 1950s and 1960s, it did deliver on that promise, especially in North America, Europe, and Japan. The benefits to other parts of the world were far less widespread, but still significant in some cases. Each generation enjoyed higher standards of living than the previous one. Infant mortality came down, and life expectancy grew. More people had access to education. The liberal state of affairs was repeatedly challenged by recurrent economic crises, although none of them as profound and long-lasting in its effects as the Great Depression after 1929 or the Great Recession after 2008. This last crisis focused attention on the extent to which technological change and economic and financial globalization had generated inequality and dualism across the world. It exposed the failure of technocratic policy recipes, and provided fertile soil for the growth of nationalist populism.

But most importantly, the 2008 crisis shook the very foundations of liberalism by exposing its biases and contradictions. First and foremost, the crisis undermined the position of the middle classes in societies. Paradoxically, the middle class grew in size and wealth in emerging economies while it stagnated in the rich countries. A second key development was the concentration of wealth. By 2015, the top 1 percent of the world's population owned more wealth than the rest of us combined. Third, the crisis put the welfare state more on the defensive than ever before. Saddled by large levels of debt, governments resorted to cutting services. In turn, this development meant that parties on the left were deprived of their most important electoral card. Throughout Europe, social democratic parties lost most of their base of support. Meanwhile, on the right, moderate parties lost ground to new anti-immigration and antiglobalization political formations as voters looked for scapegoats.

As if the hollowing out of the middle class and the breakdown of traditional political parties and alignments were not enough, technology disrupted industries and eliminated jobs in both the manufacturing and service sectors. Technological change was perhaps responsible for as many as three in four manufacturing jobs lost in Europe and the United States. Meanwhile, in the developing world, technology was adopted enthusiastically by both middle class and poor people. Astonishingly, as of 2013 nearly 1.5 billion people in the world had access to a mobile phone but not to a working toilet.[1] Bypassing previous technological waves has enabled some developing countries to be at the forefront of new technology adoption. For instance, a far greater proportion of the population in Kenya used mobile payments than in Europe or the United States.

As consequential as these built-in biases were, the biggest problem with the liberal order had to do with its internal contradictions. From the beginning, the post–World War II Global Liberal Order included a certain measure of dialectical incongruity. Economic liberalism has always transgressed boundaries in that the logic of the free market implies eliminating cross-national barriers and relegating sovereignty to the background. By contrast, political liberalism depends on a certain definition of citizenship, which requires drawing boundaries and establishing borders. It is precisely the blurring of national borders as a result of migration, trade, capital flows, technology, and other forces that lie at the center of current political and economic debates. These issues became even more pronounced as the world moved from Version 1.0 to Version 2.0 of the Global Liberal Order.

Who Stands by the Global Liberal Order?

As of 2017 it was hard to find vocal supporters or defenders of the Global Liberal Order. On the left, movements such as Occupy Wall Street and its equivalents in Europe, the electoral strength of Senator Bernie Sanders, and the rise of anticapitalist political parties in Greece, Spain, and elsewhere have prompted the traditional labor-based parties to move away from the center of the political spectrum in search for votes. Meanwhile, on the right the entire liberal agenda has come under attack for its permissive stance on immigration and unfulfilled promises regarding jobs. While right-of-center parties in Britain and France, for instance, have not made any ideological compromises to gain votes, they saw their electoral space shrink as a result of the rise of the UK Independence Party and the Front National, respectively. Meanwhile, in Germany and Spain the ruling conservatives have managed thus far to defuse any challenge on their policies coming from the right.

It is unprecedented to see that the only two countries that unconditionally support the Global Liberal Order at international summit meetings are China and Germany. At some level, it is easy to see why. Both enjoy large trade surpluses, and both stand to benefit from a continued emphasis on free trade. At the same time, they make only a minor contribution to the diplomatic and security infrastructure required to sustain it. Having said that, they make an odd couple, and, unlike Britain and the United States of decades past, they do not coordinate their policies or their actions. In fact, Germany does not have a free hand in the sense that it is ultimately responsible for the continuity and well-being of the European Union and the Euro Zone, commitments that constrain her policy and diplomatic choices. China, for its part, benefits from the economic and financial aspects of the Global Liberal Order, but is not interested in its political dimension. In fact, it appears to be flatly opposed to it.

At the Davos and G20 meetings in 2017 it seemed as if China and Germany had become the de facto leaders of the world. They have become the advocates of the Global Liberal Order at such gatherings, defending the virtues of not only free trade and free capital flows but also of the Paris climate change accord. Germany continues to insist on open borders and a welcoming attitude toward refugees. In the absence of U.S. leadership, the EU and Japan announced a new trade deal. While the Trump administration shuts itself out of global forums, China convened thirty heads of state in Beijing to mark the launching of their "Belt and Road" infrastructure initiative, in which China intends to invest at least $4 trillion. That is a massive amount by any measure. By comparison, the Marshall Plan amounted to about $160 billion in today's dollars. India is also embarking on an economic path that makes it a full participant in the global economy. As the world's largest democracy, it is also one of the youngest emerging markets, meaning that in the future it may well become the largest consumer market, surpassing China not only in total population but also purchasing power. It has become readily apparent that, with or without U.S. participation, the most important economies in the world intend to preserve most of the Global Liberal Order Version 2.0.

The uncertainty that Trump's election has cast over the Global Liberal Order is compounded by the deeds and words of China's leader, Xi Jinping, which seem to oscillate between liberal and antiliberal. Xi is someone who defies easy categorization. He has been labelled "a 'weak leader,' a 'consensus builder,' a hardcore conservative, 'a closet liberal' or even 'China's Gorbachev.'"[2] He has moved swiftly to consolidate his personal power, dismantling China's system of collective rule. The observation that he is antiliberal in all political matters internal to China but liberal in everything that has to do with the economy is an oversimplification. For instance, while he has promoted policies to place the private sector at the core of the Chinese economy, he has continued to support national champions (i.e., state-owned companies). He is also a staunch protectionist when it comes to the service sector and, especially, everything relating to the digital economy, where China is poised to become a leading global player.

Politically, Xi appears to be antiliberal, but he has appointed many U.S.-trained technocrats to key positions. He has certainly cracked down on dissent, both in China and in Hong Kong, and simultaneously has sought to eradicate corruption within the Communist Party and the government bureaucracy at the national and provincial levels, perhaps a move to strengthen his power more than to respond to social demands for change. Echoing the Monroe Doctrine, he has claimed "Asia for Asians," and observed that "the Pacific Ocean is vast enough to embrace both China and the United States."[3]

To be fair, governing China is a hard balancing act. The country is extremely diverse and is changing fast. Inequality between rural and urban areas, and within the big cities, has skyrocketed. The government faces opposition to its rule in two-fifths of its territory, especially Tibet and the western provinces. It must deliver strong economic growth so that more people are lifted out of poverty and the middle class continues to see its fortunes soar. The government has to manage an economic transition not just from state industry to the free market but from low-wage manufacturing to higher-value-added activities. It needs to keep an eye on its deeply flawed banking sector, and at the same time ensure that the bourgeoning private sector does not falter.

Globally, China has pursued an aggressive policy of investment in Africa, the Middle East, and Latin America. But in Asia, Chinese maritime expansion has met with distrust or outright opposition by its neighbors. China has outstanding territorial or maritime disputes with each of them. And in North Korea, China faces an insoluble problem in that it prefers to have a nuclear-armed neighbor as a friend than as a foe, thus making any strong actions against the Kim Jong-un regime unlikely.

China's increasing success at establishing economic and financial ties throughout the developing world does not bode well for the future of liberalism. Increasingly, governments see China as a nimble dealmaker that attaches few, if any, political or moral strings. Chinese firms, mostly from the state-owned sector, have invested tens of billions of dollars each year in South America, sub-Saharan Africa, Central Asia, East and Southeast Asia, and the Arab World. Similar amounts have reached Europe, the United States, and Australia, a country that China sees as strategically important. China has become the most important trading partner for most economies in East Asia and for several in Africa and South America. China is interested in free trade and investment, but many of the deals secured by its companies fall under the category of "managed deals" and "managed trade" as opposed to the classic arm's-length arrangements that we associate with liberal trade. Countries attracted to the Chinese economic and financial orbit no longer see the benefits of both economic and political liberalism, given that China is a champion of the former but not the latter. This poses a grave threat to how the world might view the virtues of liberalism in all of its dimensions.

The other wild card in the future evolution of the Global Liberal Order involves India. Like China, it promises to reshape the global economy by its sheer size. India boasts some of the most vibrant entrepreneurial and technological success stories of all time, from information technology to pharmaceuticals, and from steel to financial services. In 2014 India stunned the world by putting a satellite in Mars's orbit at the first attempt, and at a cost of just $74 million. (By comparison, the movie *Gravity* cost $130 million to produce.) Most critically, India has a young population, and by 2040 will most likely have a bigger domestic consumer market than China's, making it the largest in the world.

India is, however, a study in contradictions perhaps like no other country. It is the world's largest democracy, but lawlessness, corruption, poverty, and discrimination are rampant. Many groups, especially women and children, feel defenseless across vast swaths of the country. It is perhaps the most diverse nation-state in the world in terms of religion, ethnicity, caste, and language. India ranks toward the bottom in terms of freedom of the press, at about the same level as Jordan and Venezuela, and not that much better than Russia or Turkey. And yet, there it is. Parties alternate in power. Leaders come and go through democratic elections. The economy grows, and the middle class is expanding.

While the long-term future of the Global Liberal Order depends on U.S. leadership, China's and India's posture will be an increasingly determining factor. Both countries stand to benefit from continued liberal economic and demographic flows. China's economy cannot do well without access to raw materials and markets around the world. India is less reliant on exports, although increasingly so. Free movement of peoples has benefited it and constitutes a major advantage in the future, as more entrepreneurial and technological activities in the world become mediated by ethnic networks and diasporas.

And yet, these two countries could not be more different. At some point, the future of the world will depend on what types of principles and rules of international collaboration they each espouse. Some kind of accommodation between the two Asian powerhouses will be necessary for stability to be the norm in the world. They both have experienced the benefits of liberalism through the lens of economic growth. But both continue to promote, or tolerate, gigantic state-controlled apparatuses that are a constant source of corruption and inefficiency. And both still face the formidable task of raising hundreds of millions of people out of poverty.

The rising economic and financial clout of China around the world, and to a lesser extent India, has not been matched by a corresponding increase in military presence. During the nineteenth century, the Royal Navy controlled the seas and enforced liberal rules about investment and trade, which tended to benefit the British. After World War II, the United States took over, and American workers and companies also took advantage of their country's leading position as the Western global power. With the collapse of the Soviet Union, American military might has become even more salient as United States is the only country with the ability to project force around the globe, spending on its military more than the rest of the world combined. Two observations about the military role of the United States are worth making in the wake of the populist and nationalist backlash. If American foreign policy were to continue turning isolationist, it is not clear what purpose such a large worldwide military presence would serve. However, it would be rather anachronistic, controversial, and illegitimate for China to take over in order to preserve a liberal economic order without also promoting political liberalism. Regardless of that issue, as the historian Paul Kennedy once argued, the United States may actually be approaching a situation of "imperial overstretch," whereby its global security and defense commitments exceed its ability to fund the large and sophisticated military required.[4] That eventuality could materialize sooner if the dollar were to lose its preeminent place in the global financial architecture.

The Changing of the Guard: From the Dollar to the Renminbi

Prominent among the issues affecting the immediate future of the Global Liberal Order Version 2.0 is the future of international currencies. It carries many potential repercussions beyond the world of finance and the economy. It is a political and a geopolitical issue as well.

It is unlikely that the Global Liberal Order will survive without an alternative to the dollar. The reason is that the dollar was never designed to be the world's *leading* international currency. It played that role rather successfully between 1944 and 1971, when it was convertible into gold. In the wake of large deficits and inflation, President Nixon decided to do away with the peg, a move that ushered in a period of currency instability worldwide. As Ronald I. McKinnon put it in *The Unloved Dollar Standard*,

> the world dollar standard is an accident of history that greatly facilitates international trade and exchange.

Although the strong network effects of the dollar standard greatly increase the financial efficiency of multilateral trade, nobody loves it. Erratic U.S. monetary and exchange policies since the late 1960s have made, and still make, foreigners unhappy [. . .] It is a remarkable survivor that is too valuable to lose and too difficult to replace.[5]

With a free-floating dollar, some currencies gained ground while others lost it. The dollar itself went through periods of steep devaluation, especially after the Plaza Accord of 1985, a phase of decline that lasted from the early 1970s until 1995. It then gained in value relative to a trade-weighted basket of currencies until 2002, when it fell again at a time of rapidly expanding deficits. It took the uncertainty of the Great Recession in 2008 for the dollar to change course again, this time propelled upward as the only sizable financial safe haven in the world (in spite of having been the currency of the economy that caused the problem in the first place). But by early 2009 the dollar was again in decline, a cycle that lasted until mid-2011. Since then the dollar has mostly tended to appreciate.

These swings in the value of the dollar were not minor. They amounted to plus or minus 30 to 40 percent fluctuations, wide enough to affect global patterns of trade and competitiveness. Most importantly, the dollar is the leading reserve currency, accounting for nearly 64 percent of all allocated reserves, followed by the euro at almost 20 percent. Most analysts and economists agree that the dollar is not intrinsically a strong currency, given large deficits, but there is no viable alternative to it. As the economist Edwar Prasad asks, "If not the dollar, then what?"

And he continues: "This is not a story about American exceptionalism. Rather, it is one about weaknesses in the rest of the world and deep problems in the structure of the global monetary system."[6] At the same time, there are existential doubts about the future of the euro, and the other junior reserve currencies are not in a position to attract more reserves either because of their own weaknesses (e.g., pound sterling, yen) or because the issuing country is not large enough to offer the vast amounts of reserve assets required (Australian dollar, Canadian dollar, Swiss franc).

Most importantly, the stability of the Global Liberal Order cannot be sustained unless there is a changing of the guard. "The United States cannot escape the inherent logic of demography and convergence," argues Arvind Subramanian, an economist with experience at the IMF and GATT. In order for the inevitable dominance of China to be derailed, "not just will the United States have to grow substantially faster than the long-run trend but it must be seen as strong fiscally and, above all, able to reverse the pall of economic and social stagnation that has enveloped its middle class."[7]

The first indications of a major transition are already visible. As of 2014, nearly one-third of China's trade was being settled in renminbi, although 80 percent of it had to do with Hong Kong. This proportion has dropped during the last two years to about 11 percent due to the renminbi's devaluation and stiffer capital controls. These issues highlight how much work remains to be done for the renminbi to become a major international currency. Meanwhile, the proportion of foreign direct investment settled in renminbi has skyrocketed in recent years to over

80 percent. East Asian countries have started to track the renminbi as opposed to the dollar, a move that started with renminbi appreciation after the 2008 crisis and continued with its depreciation since 2014. The renminbi became in 2013 the second most important currency for trade finance after the dollar, with an 8.7 percent share of letters of credit and collections compared to 81.1 percent for the dollar. The so-called dim-sum bond market for renminbi-denominated bonds issued outside China has grown considerably since its inception in 2007, although it is still an "off-shore" operation. While the renminbi is the seventh most widely used currency for international payments, it represents less than 2 percent of the total, and much of it has to do with the transactions between Chinese companies and their Hong Kong subsidiaries. In spite of the dim-sum bonds, China has only made about $300 billion of renminbi-denominated assets available to foreign investors, compared to the $56 trillion denominated in U.S. dollars, $29 trillion in euros, and $17 trillion in yen. The Chinese renminbi became a reserve currency in the last quarter of 2016, although accounting for just over 1 percent of the world's total.[8]

Obviously, it makes sense for the renminbi to become a major reserve currency in the future. China is the world's largest trading power, and it will become the largest economy within a few years. But investors need to have trust in the renminbi, something that so far has proven elusive. The currency is not convertible, and its value is determined by the government. Moreover, capital flows are not liberalized, and the legal system is not especially prepared to protect investors. As the leading expert on these issues has noted,

China faces significant challenges as it pursues renminbi internationalization. While China may be a large economy, it remains a poor one. Its financial markets lack depth and liquidity. Encouraging international use of the renminbi will require substantial liberalization of the current account, in the course of which many things can go wrong. As growth slows, China will face economic, political and social tensions. There may then be pressure for officials to slow or reverse the external financial liberalization, state enterprise [. . .] Finally, China's political system may be an obstacle to renminbi internationalization. Foreigners will feel comfortable holding financial instruments in China only if they believe that their investments are secure.[9]

One very important series of steps toward achieving internationalization of the renminbi involves making Chinese government bonds available to investors at offshore financial centers like London and Hong Kong. In May 2017 a joint announcement between the People's Bank of China and the Hong Kong Monetary Authority accelerated this prospect by creating "Bond Connect," a set of new mechanisms to facilitate investment in both directions.[10] Hong Kong offers China a world-class financial center with all of the desirable institutions that foreigners like to see before investing. The Hong Kong dollar is fully convertible, investors enjoy the benefits of free capital flows, its banking system has long operated under open conditions, the British left behind a sound legal system based on common law, the city is home to a large and vibrant securities market, policy making is predictable, the government is fiscally responsible, the English language is widely spoken, and there is a large expatriate community working in financial services. It is impressive that Hong Kong's stock market is the sixth largest in the world by market capitalization after the NYSE, Nasdaq, Tokyo, LSE, and Euronext. In addition, Hong Kong is a major source and destination of foreign direct investment (FDI), ranking as the second-largest outward investor in the world with a cumulative stock of $1.5 trillion as of the end of 2015, up from just $12 billion in 1990, and also as the second-largest recipient of FDI, with just above $1.6 trillion in 2015, up from $202 billion in 1990 and trailing only the United States. Most of these large amounts have to do with the activities of companies from mainland China and other countries that use Hong Kong as a financial platform. Thus, Hong Kong is already playing a key role in the internationalization of the Chinese economy, although the duality of domestic and offshore renminbi deposits, assets, and transactions creates distortions that could hinder the modernization of China's domestic financial sector.

Toward a Global Liberal Order Version 3.0

Version 2.0 has run its course. It is time for a software update. The world has moved well beyond the realities and historical contingencies that motivated Thatcher, Reagan, and Clinton to reform the Global Liberal Order that Truman and his British counterparts established after World War II. Today's world is one of technological opportunity and promise, one in which emerging markets are lifting people out of poverty at astonishing rates. But it is also a world in which many feel left behind, the environment is deteriorating, and the clock is ticking with climate change. Four areas need the world's immediate attention.

Harnessing the Energy of Popular Movements

Perhaps one of the biggest mistakes made by those who support the Global Liberal Order is to take it for granted. Meanwhile, popular movements have proliferated on the left and the right. Some of them have been true grassroots movements, including the antiglobalization movement during the 1990s and 2000s, or the short-lived Occupy Wall Street. Others have been funded by politically motivated actors, and thus departed from the grassroots model, with the U.S. Tea Party as the clearest example. Trump frequently refers to his base as a movement, and it has many features consistent with that characterization. Senator Bernie Sanders also struck a chord with a large number of voters disenchanted with the new Democratic politics.

The Global Liberal Order cannot regain the broad consensus that once supported it without redirecting the energy of popular movements toward a defense of individual liberties and economic principles carrying the potential of benefiting a large segment of the population. It seems clear that rising inequality, as a result in part of the implementation of Version 2.0, undermined the traditional arguments in favor of liberalism. In fact, the term *neoliberalism* has been used indiscriminately to criticize the supporters of Version 2.0, accusing them of having turned against the interests of poor people and of the working class in favor of the financial elites.

In the United States, it is certainly true that the growth of the financial economy continued unabated during Democratic administrations. In fact, during the 1990s the Clinton administration promoted substantial deregulation of the financial services sector. Tellingly, Hillary Clinton's ties to Wall Street made her an easy target for both Sanders and Trump during the 2016 U.S. presidential election.

Liberals have two options if they wish to regain the initiative and win over the minds and hearts of those who feel displaced. The first requires doing a much better job at explaining why Version 2.0 is superior to Version 1.0. Such explanations would need to be substantiated by evidence that the Global Liberal Order reduces inequality, at least by raising all boats. The second would acknowledge that Version 2.0 does not work as intended, and open a debate as to the design of Version 3.0. As of 2017, leftist critics of the Global Liberal Order were obsessed with imposing barriers on free trade, while those on the right were adamant that international migration be curtailed at all costs. Neither recipe is acceptable in principle to true liberals, but there must be some room for political compromise.

In the United States the fragmentation of liberal political factions played out powerfully during the 2010s, leading to the 2016 presidential election. The New Deal liberals presented themselves as the true defenders of working-class values and interests, against the claims of both Donald Trump and the corporate-friendly Democratic liberals with ties to Wall Street. Caught in the cross-fire, the latter had a difficult time attracting displaced blue-collar workers to their platform. New Deal liberals tend to forget that even Franklin Delano Roosevelt was against protectionism, and that the United States was a champion of free trade and investment during the heyday of labor union influence in the 1950s and early 1960s. As the liberal commentator Jonathan Chait has noted, "rising international competition made business owners more ruthless, civil rights spawned a forty-year white backlash against government, and antigovernment extremists captured the Republican Party, destroying the bipartisan basis for progressive legislation that had once allowed Eisenhower to expand Social Security and Nixon to create the Environmental Protection Agency."[11]

At the core of the problem with American politics lies the feeling on the left, and especially among participants in grassroots movements, that the new Democratic Party of Clinton and Obama is no different than the Republican Party because both are pro-market, antilabor, and servile to Wall Street. Both are accused of being neoliberal. Meanwhile, conservative Republicans have made a huge effort to persuade people that "liberal" is the equivalent of "left-wing extremism," especially when it comes to social policy. In fact, Bernie Sanders seemed to thrive among voters self-identifying as liberal and progressive. To make matters even more confusing, the term *neoconservative* or *neocon* came to describe the most extreme and hawkish elements in the Bush administration after 9/11. How has it become possible that neoliberals can be both moderate, centrist Democrats who betrayed the working class but believe in higher taxes to take care of social programs, and hard-core Republicans, many of them neocons, who flatly oppose such proposals favoring instead lower taxes and retrograde social policies? As Jonathan Cheit put it, this position obscures "the large gulf between Newt Gingrich and Bill Clinton, Paul Ryan and Barack Obama."[12]

If that were not enough, Donald Trump's denunciation of neocon interventionist foreign policy, adamant antiglobalization agenda, and populist politics throws the political situation into utter chaos by challenging the Left's monopoly as the champions of the working class. Meanwhile, Bernie Sanders launched the most powerful critique of Democratic politics, offering an alternative modelled after the Canadian or European leftist parties based in the labor movement and the principles of social democracy. He was certainly successful at energizing a movement on the left. The question for the future is whether the popular movements yearning for progressive policies can ever succeed by themselves or if they need to find common ground with the Democrats they accuse of being neoliberal.

In general, the prefix "neo-" became a way of conveying a more intense strand of liberalism or of conservatism when in fact the prefix "hyper-" would have been more accurate, as in "hyperliberalism" or "hyperconservatism." Rather than labeling Version 2.0 of the Global Liberal Order as hyperliberal, however, what makes it different from Version 1.0 is that it tilted the balance between economic and political liberalism in favor of the former. Free markets, including financial markets and financial flows, took precedence over political considerations. In fact, the technocratic origins of Version 2.0 reveal an intention to subordinate the political to economic principles. Part of this agenda included the idea that governments needed to be reined in by the markets. This vision was operationalized by making governments dependent on financing through one of the largest markets in the world, the market for government securities. Investors in government bonds gained the upper hand at the turn of the century by demanding higher yields.

It seems clear that for liberalism to regain the initiative and build a social and political base of support, the functioning balance between political liberalism and economic liberalism needs to be reestablished. The arguments to bring back into the liberal coalition citizens who have joined alternative movements on the right and the left must emphasize liberal values and practices in the political realm. Appealing to them on the basis of a better economic future might not be enough given how much Version 2.0 has undermined the credibility of liberalism. Specifically, technocratic arguments about the best way to organize and regulate markets, or to formulate economic policies, are likely to fall on deaf ears among those who feel cheated by the economic and financial elites.

Political Engagement and Participation

An overhaul and rejuvenation of the Global Liberal Order will be hard without an active process of democratic participation. The quality of democratic life, however, is on the decline in some parts of the world once proud of their political achievements, while it is inadequate or simply does not exist in some of the most rapidly growing economies. The shocking rise of nationalist and populist parties and candidates would not have taken place without the indifference and inaction of large parts of the electorate in Europe and the United States. Young and middle-aged urban people alike, both educated and not, continue to exhibit lower turnout rates than the groups that have provided most of the support for populist, antitrade, and xenophobic parties and candidates. It seems as if the crumbling of the Global Liberal Order has been driven primarily by those who should be its most ardent champions. Liberalism cannot survive if people are not motivated to be politically engaged, and to vote.

The politicians and technocrats who implemented the Global Liberal Order did a great job at it in some respects, but ultimately failed to appreciate and arrest the negative undercurrents, especially concerning Version 2.0. Footloose financial globalization and technological change left large segments of the population behind, people who did not have the motivation or the skills to ride the putative wave of progress. In fact, progress eluded many people, who felt excluded, and rightly so. On both sides of the Atlantic, social cohesion was undermined by wealth accumulation, residential segregation, and crime. Violence erupted in Baltimore and Bobigny, while Bergen County and Billancourt thrived.

Besides the lack of effective policies to maintain social cohesion, the education sector in the United States and Europe has failed liberalism. Schools and, especially, universities have become engines of social reproduction rather than mobility. At a time of rapid technological change, one would expect the education sector to help reduce inequality. Instead, it might be exacerbating it. The liberal dream of educational access and of the knowledge-based economy has come under attack from all sides. Both liberals and antiliberals complain about the travails of education policy makers and administrators, pointing out their inability to prepare people of all ages for the challenges of our time.

In fact, traditional politicians and policy makers have been labeled by the antiliberal populists as elitist. They have been accused of being out of touch with reality, oblivious to the daily problems afflicting ordinary people. As an act of defiance, and in some cases desperation, they have given their support to political opportunists espousing quick fixes to complicated problems. Simplistic messages resonate with a segment of the electorate tired of unfulfilled promises, rising inequality, and corruption scandals. The shortening of the news cycle and the controversy over fake news has made it possible for a new class of politicians, with no shortage of demagogues among them, to challenge the political establishment and the traditional political parties.

One avenue to regain the quality of democratic life in Western Europe and the United States might be to implement the concept of "deliberative democracy," which entails engaging people as decision makers and not just as voters. The promise of this approach lies in its emphasis on avoiding polarization by combining the principles of representative and direct notions of democracy. One of the key challenges to the Global Liberal Order is the lack of consensus over the basic building blocks of a free society and economy as partisanship has grown. Another is the distrust that a large segment of the electorate has developed toward scientific knowledge and experts.

Meanwhile, the quality of democratic life has not just worsened but almost completely disappeared in many African, Latin American, Middle-Eastern, and Asian countries. Those peculiar combinations of democratic and authoritarian traits we call anocracies have become far too common in global affairs. The cases of Russia and Turkey are especially problematic because of their pivotal role in their spheres of influence. While we have fewer dictatorships than ever, the world's largest trading nation, and soon-to-become largest economy, happens to be one of them. It remains to be seen if the world can function properly under some renovated version of the Global Liberal Order under the circumstances.

What to Do about International Capital Flows?

If Version 3.0 of the Global Liberal Order were to address one specific problem inherited from Version 2.0, the best candidate would be international capital flows, the source of much dispute, disruption, and discontent. Economists argue that regulation makes sense when there is evidence of distortions such as imperfect information that might make markets work improperly. As economic historian Barry Eichengreen has observed, capital markets are beset by two specific information problems, namely, adverse selection (the least creditworthy individuals, firms, or governments always prefer to borrow more), and moral hazard (borrowers are willing to assume additional risk if they suspect there is enough financing to rescue them if they get into trouble). The 2008 crisis offers ample evidence of both problems. In addition, he argues, international capital flows can generate negative externalities, i.e., costs to society, because when a country in financial disarray faces outflows of capital, foreign investors will sell domestic assets and the exchange rate will depreciate. That in turn will make the country's difficulties even bigger.[13] As we saw in a previous chapter, IMF economists have concluded that short-term capital flows can increase the probability of currency and banking crises.[14] In addition, large capital inflows may create bubbles and undermine the competitiveness of the recipient country's exports because of the appreciation of the real (i.e., inflation adjusted) exchange rate. Lastly, it is not possible for a country committed to free capital flows to simultaneously maintain a stable exchange rate and have its own monetary policy. This is known as the "impossible trinity." Policy makers (and politicians) typically prefer to exercise monetary discretion, meaning that the exchange rate must fluctuate if capital flows are free, oftentimes hurting the country's competitiveness.

If international capital flows come together with information imperfections and negative externalities, why do so many economists and policy makers reject capital controls? Such controls might include a tax on foreigners' purchases of domestic assets, a withholding tax on interest and capital gains, a requirement to maintain a non-interest-bearing deposit equal to a certain percentage of the amount invested by foreigners, or a tollgate tax on short-term capital outflows. Historically, many economies have implemented capital controls, including the United States, most European countries, China (unsurprisingly), Brazil, Thailand, South Korea, and even free-market enthusiast Chile, to name but a few. Many of them continue to use these controls today.

One famous idea was the Tobin Tax, proposed in 1972 by Nobel laureate James Tobin shortly after the demise of the Bretton Woods system. It was essentially a tax on all spot transactions involving currency conversions.[15] He suggested a rate of approximately 0.5 percent, although without offering any calculations to show that it was the optimal level. Tobin's idea spurred much excitement among different kinds of economists, policy makers, and activists. It was oftentimes misunderstood as a tool to tax the rich and help the poor. Many countries adopted, and then dropped, different versions of a Tobin Tax. The UN and the EU also recommended similar measures at certain points. Still, the idea remains controversial and has not been implemented in any sustained way.

Opponents of capital controls argue that not allowing capital to move freely creates inefficiencies, punishes borrowers with the best ideas as to what to do with the money, rewards those who are not competitive, and can provide fertile ground for corruption. Still, there has been a movement among believers in the free market that, under certain circumstances, governments might want to deploy capital controls to buffer the economy from speculative, short-term capital flows. This position was defended by IMF staff in a 2010 paper: "If the economy is operating near potential, if the level of reserves is adequate, if the exchange rate is not undervalued, and if the flows are likely to be transitory, then use of capital controls—in addition to both prudential and macroeconomic policy—is justified as part of the policy toolkit to manage inflows."[16] Capital controls are no longer off the agenda, assuming they are transparent, reversible, reviewed frequently, and price based so as to avoid corruption and favoritism. Interestingly, the IMF also did a survey to assess the effectiveness of capital controls, finding that they tended to work as intended by policy makers seeking to reduce risks to the economy.[17] In 2011 the IMF officially issued its first-ever guidelines for using capital controls.[18]

Designing a comprehensive and balanced policy framework for the regulation of international capital flows would represent a major step toward Version 3.0 of the

Global Liberal Order, one that would have a great chance of making the global economy less prone to crises, thus contributing to higher standards of living and less inequality. Still, no consensus yet exists among policy makers.

In addition to regulating international capital flows, research indicates that there are other key firewalls when it comes to preventing economic and financial crises. The evidence for the time period between 1900 and 2009 indicates that the density of trade networks and a consolidated democratic system helps reduce the frequency of crises. Trade density means that, in response to a crisis, there are more options and channels to cope with the disruption. Consolidated democracies are more stable, and thus in a better position to deal with an economic or financial shock.[19]

What Topics Should Be on the Global Liberal Agenda?

To put it simply: the global liberal agenda should address people's problems, framing them in such a way that we can arrive at a modified Global Liberal Order that provides solutions meeting two basic requirements: they must be politically feasible and economically sound.

Climate change and environmental degradation will create numerous political and economic headaches unless they remain at the top of the agenda. The poor in the rich countries and, especially, the poor in the poorest countries stand to be the most affected by rising temperatures and continued air, soil, and water pollution. Liberalism is not just about freedom and prosperity today; it has always been committed to the long-term and to intergenerational fairness.

Free and fair trade, along with *managed* capital flows, can and should continue to be on the agenda as major engines of economic growth and development. Technology will be, nevertheless, the key economic issue as new breakthroughs occur and the creative destruction of entrepreneurship and innovation continues. Politically, there is no alternative but to take care of those who are displaced by economic and technological forces. Ignoring them creates unnecessary misery and the potential for sociopolitical upheaval.

The culture of political engagement must be nurtured if liberalism is to survive and its benefits delivered. Many of the shocking votes of the last few years could have turned out differently with broader political participation. Tuning out is never the best answer, especially when opportunistic politicians are roaming the landscape.

The collapse of the Global Liberal Order would result in a walled world, with protectionist barriers keeping foreign goods at bay while brick and mortar (or barbed wire) seal borders against immigration. Travel and tourism might become harder, and prices for consumer goods would tend to rise. Ironically, the incentives for further automation might well rise as companies scramble to keep prices low, displacing ever larger numbers of workers. Geopolitical conflicts over market access and natural resources would likely flare up. For consumers, the choice is as stark as it can be: either Farage or *fromage*. For voters, the choice will also be clear: either Le Pen or *le bon sens*. For the entire world, including the United States, the decision involves siding with Truman under a Version 3.0, or with Trump.

These would be the considerations that might lead to a Version 3.0 of the Global Liberal Order, an improved international arrangement to provide for stability and prosperity:

- An understanding that *both* markets and governments are needed to realize the promises of liberalism. While Version 1.0 struck a workable balance between them, Version 2.0 tilted it in favor of markets to an excessive degree. A new Version 3.0 needs to find another balance for the present realities confronting the world, especially those having to do with technological change and social inequality.
- An informed debate about the economic benefits and the social costs of free trade, ranged against the dangers of protectionism. Protectionism as a rule leads to lagging innovation, entrenched interest groups, and consumer losses. Under very specific circumstances, protectionism may make sense, but only if the mechanism for removing the protectionist measures is in place before they come into force. Having said that, no free trade policy should be a stand-alone initiative. It must be underpinned by a firm commitment and a long-term strategy to provide for the needs of those displaced by trade. Absent such compensatory schemes, we run the risk of a continued political backlash and the exorbitant economic and social costs of dooming certain groups of workers and communities to decline.
- A realization that a system of capital controls might reduce the probability of crises occurring when outflows increase, minimize their effect on inequality, and leave governments with enough room for maneuver. The government's ability to formulate economic policies cannot be undermined, especially in the most

vulnerable economies. As in the case of free trade, the liberal approach is to reject both extremes, namely, total governmental discretion and zero autonomy.

- A recognition of the transformational role of technology and of its ill effects on people caught off guard by the process of creative destruction. Technological change has demonstrated time and again that it brings the best and the worst out of the capitalist economy. While the free market seems to do a great job at providing the incentives for innovation, the social and political costs cannot be ignored. One cannot expect society to absorb all of the so-called externalities, namely, the side effects or collateral damage.

- An appreciation of the contribution of immigrants to the healthy and dynamic transformation of the society and the economy, noting that they tend not to directly compete with locals for jobs. The ideals of liberalism include the right of people to seek a better life, especially when confronted by political persecution or war in their home country. The reality of vast demographic imbalances in the world, however, represents a stark reminder that totally free movements of people might become unmanageable. Collaboration between high-fertility (typically developing) and low-fertility (usually rich) countries is essential to striking a balance between completely open borders and building walls.

- Respect for the liberal principle that everyone is endowed with political rights and for the idea that the government must protect them. This principle includes the obligation of the government to enable all citizens to exercise their political rights, thus to facilitate political participation and deliberation. In this vein, voter intimidation, voter suppression, and election meddling are practices that need to be eradicated. Liberalism cannot possibly work without political inclusion.

- A recognition that Europe and the United States can no longer attempt by themselves to steer the global economy and the international system of states. The demographic and economic balance in the world has shifted, and so must governance structures and decision making. Isolationism must be avoided, as liberal and not-so-liberal states in the world jockey for position in the midst of large-scale transformations in the economy and the society, and in the realm of technology.

The future of liberalism in politics and economics hinges to a very large extent on making the distinction between "illiberal" and "antiliberal," and on persuading people that those are two very different concepts. In many ways, the antiliberal leftist grassroots movements of Europe and the United States are not illiberal in their political beliefs, especially their political proposals. They ask for political freedoms, for a level playing field, for tolerance and support for minorities, including ethnic minorities and the LGBT community. They are more likely to be illiberal when it comes to economic matters, while those on the right are more inclined to back illiberal political ideas, especially about immigration. The case of Trump poses a challenge in this respect, because his staunchest followers (his "base"), seem to support illiberal ideas and policies regarding both politics and the economy. The key point is that much of the discontent is directed not at liberal ideas, principles, and policies themselves but at the agents of liberalism, especially the economic, business, financial, and cultural elites so detested by the radical Left and the Far Right. Thus, at least some of the resistance among people who typically occupy the political mainstream to support and advance liberal proposals nowadays might disappear if the political and economic establishment renews and reinvents itself. That would leave significant, but not decisive, numbers of people at either end of the political spectrum still dissatisfied, and it would certainly be a mistake to ignore them. But such a "recentering" of politics in Europe and the United States would go a long way to overcome the present divisions, and to give liberal ideas another chance.

In spite of these rays of hope, the world may still evolve in a direction different than liberalism. This may bring some short-term gains, to certain groups, segments, or countries. If political and economic liberalism are to survive, compromises will need to be made and tradeoffs will need to be adjudicated. The main advantage of liberalism is that it provides a flexible framework for governments, businesses, workers, and citizens to interact and deliberate in a way that they can explore and make necessary compromises. It is precisely the apparent opposition of political and economic liberalism that provides for a dynamic of change. For it is clear that as the world changes, the only possible response is change itself. It is hard to imagine how the alternatives—nationalism, populism, isolationism, authoritarianism—can lead to a better future, except in a narrow, short-sighted, and parochial sense. Liberalism stands alone as the only framework with the potential to provide for inclusive prosperity, assuming we manage to tame its tendency to benefit those at the top and to destroy as well as create, as it seeks to lift everyone up.

Notes

Chapter 1

1. Truman Doctrine (1947). https://history.state.gov/milestones/1945-1952/truman-doctrine

2. Ira Katznelson, *Fear Itself: The New Deal and the Origins of Our Time* (New York: W. W. Norton, 2013).

3. Thomas Philippon and Ariell Reshef, "An International Look at the Growth of Modern Finance," *Journal of Economic Perspectives* 27, no. 2 (Spring 2013): 73–96.

4. Barry Eichengreen, *Hall of Mirrors: The Great Depression, the Great Recession, and the Uses—and Misuses—of History* (New York: Oxford University Press, 2015), 204–5.

5. As quoted by Stephen Labaton, "A New Financial Era," *New York Times*, October 23, 1999, section A, 1.

6. Quoted in Barry Eichengreen, *Exorbitant Privilege* (New York: Oxford University Press, 2011), 103.

7. Ibid.; Raghuram Rajan, *Fault Lines: How Hidden Fractures Still Threaten the World Economy* (Princeton, NJ: Princeton University Press, 2010).

8. Nathaniel Nash, "Treasury Now Favors the Creation of Huge Banks." *New York Times*, June 7, 1987.

9. Sandra L. Suarez and Robin Kolodny, "Paving the Road to 'Too Big to Fail': Business Interests and the Politics of Financial Deregulation in the U.S.," *Politics & Society* 39 (2011): 74–102.

10. Ibid.

11. Rawi Abdelal, *Capital Rules: The Construction of Global Finance* (Cambridge, MA: Harvard University Press, 2007).

12. Dani Rodrik, "Goodbye Washington Consensus, Hello Washington Confusion?" *Journal of Economic Literature* (December 2006): 973–87.

13. Ibid.

14. http://rtais.wto.org/UI/PublicAllRTAList.aspx

15. Abdelal, *Capital Rules*, 56–59.

16. Eichengreen, *Exorbitant Privilege*, 70, 130.

17. Kevin H. O'Rourke and Alan M. Taylor, "Cross of Euros," *Journal of Economic Perspectives* 27, no. 3 (Summer 2013): 178.

18. Abdelal, *Capital Rules*, 65–71.

19. Quoted in Eichengreen, *Hall of Mirrors*, 90.

20. Abdelal, *Capital Rules*, 74–77.

21. Committee for the Study of Economic and Monetary Union, *Report on Economic and Monetary Union in the European Community* (Brussels: European Community, 1989), 13.

22. Abdelal, *Capital Rules*, 77.

23. Andrew Moravcsik, *The Choice for Europe: Social Purpose and State Power from Messina to Maastricht* (Ithaca, NY: Cornell University Press, 1998), 435.

24. As quoted in the *Financial Times* (June 8, 2012).

25. Kenneth Dyson and Kevin Featherstone, *The Road to Maastricht: Negotiating Economic and Monetary Union* (New York: Oxford University Press, 1999), 195–99, 363–64; Moravcsik, *Choice for Europe*, 437–40.

26. Peter J. Katzenstein, "United Germany in an Integrating Europe," in *Tamed Power: Germany in Europe*, ed. Peter J. Katzenstein (Ithaca, NY: Cornell University Press, 1997), 1–48.

27. Timothy Garton Ash, "The Crisis of Europe: How the Union Came Together and Why It's Falling," *Foreign Affairs* (September–October 2012).

Chapter 2

1. A summary of the evidence appears in Mauro F. Guillén and Emilio Ontiveros, *Global Turning Points* (Cambridge: Cambridge University Press, 2016), chapter 6.

2. Ibid.

Chapter 3

1. Saskia Sassen, *Territory, Authority, Rights: From Medieval to Global Assemblages* (Princeton, NJ: Princeton University Press, 2006), 6–7.

2. Jan-Werner Müller, *What Is Populism?* (Philadelphia: University of Pennsylvania Press, 2016), 4.

3. Benedict Anderson, *Imagined Communities: Reflections on the Origin and Spread of Nationalism* (London: Verso, 1983), 6–7.

4. Matt Golder, "Far Right Parties in Europe," *Annual Review of Political Science* 19 (2016): 477–97.

5. "How Far Is Europe Swinging to the Right?" *New York Times* (March 20, 2017).

6. Golder, "Far Right Parties in Europe."

7. Daphne Halikiopoulou and Sofia Vasilopoulou, "The Rise of the Golden Dawn in Greece," in *The European Far Right: Historical and Contemporary Perspectives*, ed. Giorgos Charalambous (Nicosia: Friedrich-Ebert-Stiftung, 2015), 25.

8. Aurelien Mondon, "The Irresistible Rise of the Front National? Populism and the Mainstreaming of the Extreme Right," in *The European Far Right: Historical and Contemporary Perspectives*, ed. Giorgos Charalambous (Nicosia: Friedrich-Ebert-Stiftung, 2015), 39.

9. Krisztian Szabados, "The Particularities and Uniqueness of Hungary's Jobbik," in *The European Far Right: Historical and Contemporary Perspectives*, ed. Giorgos Charalambous (Nicosia: Friedrich-Ebert-Stiftung, 2015), 56.

10. Clara Sandelind, Mikael Hjerm, and Anna Rehnvall, "Sweden: The Immigration Country in the North," in *Nothing to Fear but Fear Itself?* (London: Demos, 2017, 405).

11. Andreas Kemper, "AfD, Pegida and the New Right in Germany," in *The European Far Right: Historical and Contemporary Perspectives*, ed. Giorgos Charalambous (Nicosia: Friedrich-Ebert-Stiftung, 2015), 43.

12. Carmen González-Enríquez, "The Spanish Exception: Unemployment, Inequality and Immigration, but No Right-Wing Populist Parties," in *Nothing to Fear but Fear Itself?* (London: Demos, 2017).

13. Ibid., 244.

14. Ibid.

15. Ivan Krastev, *After Europe* (Philadelphia: University of Pennsylvania Press, 2017), 64–71; Ivan Krastev, *Democracy Disrupted* (Philadelphia: University of Pennsylvania Press, 2014).

16. Matthew Goodwin and Caitlin Milazzo, *UKIP: Inside the Campaign to Redraw the Map of British Politics* (Oxford: Oxford University Press, 2015), 63, 126.

17. According to the Edison Exit Poll: http://www.cnn.com/election/results/exit-polls.

18. Anderson, *Imagined Communities*.

19. Hunt Allcott and Matthew Gentzkow, "Social Media and Fake News in the 2016 Election," *Journal of Economic Perspectives* 31(2) (Spring 2017): 211–36.

20. Ibid., 212.

21. Ibid., 232.

22. http://www.people-press.org/2017/07/10/sharp-partisan-divisions-in-views-of-national-institutions/.

23. http://www.journalism.org/2017/01/18/trump-clinton-voters-divided-in-their-main-source-for-election-news/.

24. Isabela Mares and Lauren Young, "Buying, Expropriating, and Stealing Votes," *Annual Review of Political Science* 19 (2016): 267–88.

25. Alan Neuhauser, "Voter Intimidation Complaints Surge," *U.S. News* (online), November 8, 2016.

26. Robert Draper, "The League of Dangerous Mapmakers," *The Atlantic* (October 2012).

27. Benjamin Highton, "Voter Identification Laws and Turnout in the United States," *Annual Review of Political Science* 20 (2017): 149–67.

28. *Assessing Russian Activities and Intentions in Recent U.S. Elections* (Washington, DC: Office of the Director of National Intelligence, 2017).

29. Uri Friedman, "Russia's Interference in the U.S. Election Was Just the Beginning," *The Atlantic*, April 26, 2017.

30. Linda Kinstler, "How to Survive a Russian Hack," *The Atlantic*, February 2, 2017.

31. Dov H. Levin, "Partisan Electoral Interventions by the Great Powers: Introducing the PEIG Dataset," *Conflict Management and Peace Science* (2016): 1–19.

32. Dov H. Levin, "When the Great Power Gets a Vote: The Effects of Great Power Electoral Interventions on Election Results," *International Studies Quarterly* 60, no. 2 (2016): 189–202.

33. Michael Sandel, "Moral Argument and Liberal Toleration: Abortion and Homosexuality," *California Law Review* 77, no. 3 (1989): 521–38; Michael Sandel, *Justice : What's the Right Thing to Do?* (New York: Farrar, Straus and Giroux, 2009); Carlos Ball, *The Morality of Gay Rights: An Exploration in Political Philosophy* (New York: Routledge, 2003).

34. Ester Boserup, *Women's Role in Economic Development* (London: Earthscan, 1970).

35. Jane S. Jaquette and Kathleen Staudt, "Women, Gender, and Development," in *Women and Gender Equity in Development Theory and Practice*, ed. Jane S. Jaquette and Gale Summerfield (Durham, NC: Duke University Press, 2006), 17–52.

Chapter 4

1. U.S. Department of Commerce, *What Is Made in America?* (Washington, DC: U.S. Department of Commerce, 2014), http://www.esa.doc.gov/sites/default/files/whatismadeinamerica_0.pdf.

2. http://www.american.edu/kogod/research/autoindex/index.cfm.

3. Robert E. Scott, *Heading South: U.S.-Mexico Trade and Job Displacement after NAFTA* (Washington, DC: Economic Policy Institute, 2011).

4. Robert W. Crandall, *The Effects of U.S. Trade Protection for Autos and Steel*, Brookings Papers on Economic Activity (1987).

5. Bureau of Labor Statistics, https://www.bls.gov/iag/tgs/iagauto.htm.

6. *Artificial Intelligence, Automation, and the Economy* (Washington, DC: Executive Office of the President, December 2016).

7. Adam Smith, *An Inquiry into the Nature and Causes of the Wealth of Nations* (Oxford: Clarendon Press, 1976), 848–49.

8. Karl Marx, *Capital* (New York: International Publishers, 1967), vol. 3, 238.

9. Jagdish Bhagwati, "The Capital Myth: The Difference between Trade in Widgets and Dollars," *Foreign Affairs* 77, no. 3 (May–June 1999): 7–12.

10. Carmen M. Reinhardt and Kenneth S. Rogoff, *This Time is Different: Eight Centuries of Financial Folly* (Princeton, NJ: Princeton University Press, 2009).

11. J. D. Ostry, P. Loungani, and D. Furceri, "Neoliberalism: Oversold?" *Finance & Development* (June 2016).

12. Davide Furceri and Prakash Loungani, "Capital Account Liberalization and Inequality," IMF Working Paper 15/243 (2015).

13. Mauro F. Guillén, *The Architecture of Collapse: The Global System in the 21st Century* (Oxford: Oxford University Press, 2016).

14. "Globalization and Inequality," in *World Economic Outlook* (Washington, DC: International Monetary Fund, 2007), 50.

15. *Annual Report on Exchange Arrangements and Exchange Restrictions* (Washington, DC: International Monetary Fund, 2016).

16. Michael Pettis, *The Great Rebalancing: Trade, Conflict, and the Perilous Road Ahead for the World Economy* (Princeton, NJ: Princeton University Press, 2013), 136.

17. Kenneth Austin, "Systemic Equilibrium in a Bretton Woods II-Type International Monetary System: The Special Roles of Reserve Issuers and Reserve Accumulators," *Journal of Post Keynesian Economics* 36, no. 4 (Summer 2014): 632.

18. Martin Wolf, *The Shifts and the Shocks: What We've Learned—and Have Still to Learn from the Financial Crisis* (New York: Penguin, 2014), 166.

19. Giovanni Peri, "Immigrants, Productivity, and Labor Markets," *Journal of Economic Perspectives* 30(4): 3–30.

20. David H. Autor, "Why Are There Still So Many Jobs?" *Journal of Economic Perspectives* 29, no. 3 (2016): 3–30; Peri, "Immigrants, Productivity, and Labor Markets."

21. National Academies of Science, Engineering and Medicine, *The Economic and Fiscal Consequences of Immigration* (Washington, DC: National Academies Press, 2017), 268.

22. Ibid., 247.

23. United Nations, *Migration Report 2015* (New York: United Nations, 2015).

24. OECD, *Is Migration Good for the Economy?* (Paris: OECD, 2014).

25. Quoted in National Academies of Science, Engineering and Medicine, *Economic and Fiscal Consequences of Immigration*, 283.

26. Ibid., 283, 316, 317.

27. Ibid., 404, 406, 462.

28. Susan K. Brown and Frank D. Bean, "Assimilation Models, Old and New: Explaining a Long-Term Process," http://www.migrationpolicy.org/article/assimilation-models-old-and-new-explaining-long-term-process.

29. Michael J. Hicks and Srikant Devaraj, *Myth and Reality of Manufacturing in America* (Muncie, IN: Center for Business and Economic Research, Ball State University, 2017).

30. Mark Muro, "Manufacturing Jobs Aren't Coming Back," *MIT Technology Review* (November 18, 2016).

31. *The Economist*, "Automation and Anxiety." https://www.economist.com/news/special-report/21700758-will-smarter-machines-cause-mass-unemployment-automation-and-anxiety.

32. FiveThirtyEight, "Trump Was Stronger Where the Economy Is Weaker," https://fivethirtyeight.com/features/trump-was-stronger-where-the-economy-is-weaker/.

33. Scott Santens, "Self-Driving Trucks Are Going to Hit Us Like a Human-Driven Truck," *Medium*, https://medium.com/basic-income/self-driving-trucks-are-going-to-hit-us-like-a-human-driven-truck-b8507d9c5961#.yl5xaqxnq.

34. *Artificial Intelligence, Automation, and the Economy*.

35. Felix Richter, "The Rise of the Sharing Economy," *Statista*, https://www.statista.com/chart/2323/the-rise-of-the-sharing-economy/.

36. David Rotman, "The 3-D Printer that Could Finally Change Manufacturing," *MIT Technology Review* (April 25, 2017).

37. Philip Boucher, Susana Nascimento, and Mihalis Kritikos, *How Blockchain Technology Could Change our Lives* (Brussels: European Union, PE 581.948, February 2017), 4.

38. Joseph A. Schumpeter, *Capitalism, Socialism and Democracy* (New York: Harper, 1975), 82.

39. "Globalization and Inequality," in *World Economic Outlook* (Washington, DC: International Monetary Fund, 2007), 49–50.

Chapter 5

1. "Deputy UN Chief Calls for Urgent Action to Tackle Global Sanitation Crisis," *UN News Centre*, March 21, 2013.

2. Cheng Li, "Understanding Xi's Contradictions," *Brookings Blog*, September 17, 2015, https://www.brookings.edu/blog/order-from-chaos /2015/09/17/understanding-xis-contradictions/.

3. Ibid.

4. Paul Kennedy, *The Rise and Fall of the Great Powers* (New York: Random House, 1987).

5. Ronald I. McKinnon, *The Unloved Dollar Standard: From Bretton Woods to the Rise of China* (New York: Oxford University Press, 2013), 3–4.

6. Eswar S. Prasad, *The Dollar Trap: How the U.S. Dollar Tightened its Grip on Global Finance* (Princeton, NJ: Princeton University Press, 2014), 11, 13.

7. Arvind Subramanian, *Eclipse: Living in the Shadow of China's Economic Dominance* (Washington, DC: Peterson Institute for International Economics, 2011), 190.

8. Citations to the sources for these data may be found in Guillén, *Architecture of Collapse*, chapter 5.

9. Barry Eichengreen, "Number One Country, Number One Currency?" *World Economy* 36, no. 4 (2013): 363–74.

10. http://www.chinabondconnect.com/en/index.htm.

11. Jonathan Cheit, "How 'Neoliberalism' Became the Left's Favorite Insult of Liberals," *New York Magazine*, July 16, 2017.

12. Ibid.

13. Barry Eichengreen, "Rethinking Capital Controls," *Milken Institute Review* (July 15, 2016).

14. Ostry, Loungani, and Furceri, "Neoliberalism: Oversold?"

15. The original proposal was made at a lecture at Princeton University in 1972, later published as James Tobin, "A Proposal for International Monetary Reform," *Eastern Economic Journal* (July–October 1978): 153–59.

16. Jonathan D. Ostry et al., "Capital Inflows: The Role of Controls," *IMF Staff Position Note* (February 19, 2010), SPN/10/04.

17. IMF, "Recent Experiences in Managing Capital Inflows" (Washington, DC: International Monetary Fund, 2011), http://www.imf .org/external/np/pp/eng/2011/021411a.pdf.

18. Sacha Dierckx, "The IMF and Capital Controls: Towards Postneoliberalism?" https://ecpr.eu/Filestore/PaperProposal/419f54b4–73ce -42cf-b3fe-4e3e6dd844d0.pdf.

19. Mauro F. Guillén, "Predicting Economic and Financial Crises: Complexity and Coupling in the Global System, 1900–2009," Working Paper (2017). Available from the author upon request.